GERM...
KEY WORDS

is a learning aid benefiting from computer analysis of 1,775,000 words. It consists of a list of the commonest two thousand words in modern written German, with their meanings in English, arranged in decreasing order of frequency, with a separate list of numerals and days of the week, and declension of a regular verb in present and imperfect. The list is divided into a hundred units averaging twenty key words each, from which many more words may be derived.

Most grammars and readers introduce words almost at random, so that a student can never be sure of mastering commonly-occurring words within a reasonable period. A frequency list such as *German Key Words* can create confidence and a sense of security in vocabulary building and, by dividing the list into manageable units, mastery can be achieved without undue strain.

Dieter Zahn has made sure that adult beginners, or pupils in the first year of secondary school, will be introduced to *all* the most frequently-occurring words in German within their first year of study. The first 1,000 words account for 83% of all word occurrences in German. An English index allows the reader to trace each word in the lists and indicates by its position the relative frequency of that word. Some students may not realise that the commonest hundred words in German include only two nouns: can you guess what they might be? The answer is given in the introduction to Dieter Zahn's *German Key Words*.

GERMAN
KEY WORDS

the basic 2,000-word vocabulary
arranged by frequency in a
hundred units

with comprehensive German and
English indexes

DIETER ZAHN

The Oleander Press

The Oleander Press
17 Stansgate Avenue
Cambridge CB2 2QZ
England

The Oleander Press
80 Eighth Avenue, Suite 303
New York,
N.Y. 10011
U.S.A.

British Library Cataloguing in Publication Data

Zahn, Dieter
German key words: the basic 2000-word
vocabulary arranged by frequency in a
hundred units with comprehensive English
and German indexes. – (Oleander language
& literature series; Vol. 17)

I. Title II. Series
433.21

ISBN 0-906672-28-7

Typeset, printed and bound in Great Britain

CONTENTS

Introduction

German Key Words has been designed as an efficient, logical, and practical computer-based word-list for anglophone learners of German in their first year and second year. It has also proved valuable as a revision tool for more advanced students.

The basic two thousand 'key' words are so called because by learning these one unlocks the door to many thousand more words: plurals from singulars, some feminines from masculines, and parts of the verb from the infinitive. Regular forms of the present tense are set out before Unit 1.

One purpose of this technique is to stimulate confidence in the learning of German by teaching the commonest words first, and leaving the less common till later. Nothing is more daunting to the beginner than finding dozens of rare words which have to be looked up in a dictionary and may not recur in reading again for several years.

German Key Words is intended to be used with a conventional grammar and a conventional dictionary, but a massive dictionary has been found in practice to unnerve the beginner, whilst most available readers introduce too early words or ideas which may be arbitrary or advanced. During this sensitive phase, when interest in learning German can be so easily encouraged or discouraged, it is suggested that the student should learn words in units of about twenty 'key' words each, thus mastering some two thousand such words by the end of the first year. Only then will she or he be ready to accumulate arbitrary words of low occurrence, many of which will in any case be related to words already learnt. Computer-based methods are by now fully familiar in mathematics and the sciences, but statistical sampling has hitherto been rarely practised in language-learning, probably because of the difficulty of establishing a sufficiently large and accurate sample to make the frequency list reliable. The Oleander Press pioneered this approach in *French Key Words* (1984) by Xavier-Yves Escande, *Italian Key Words* (1992) by Gianpaolo Intronati, *Spanish Key Words* (1993) by Pedro Casal and *Arabic Key Words* (1994) by David Quitregard.

The Units

Each of the hundred units is self-contained, Unit 1 including the twenty-or-so commonest key words, Unit 2 the next twenty commonest and so on. The key word is followed by an indication of its part of speech: *adj.*, adjective; *adv.* adverb; *conj.*, conjunction; *f.n.*, feminine noun; *interj.*, interjection; *m.n.*, masculine noun; *prep.*, preposition; *pron.*, pronoun. Verbs are not so signalled, because they are represented in each case by their infinitive, always translated beginning with 'to'.

Plurals of nouns are shown except for those ending in -*e* with the plural *n*; those ending in a consonant with the plural *e;* and those ending in -*heit, -ion, -keit, -schaft* and -*ung* ending with the plural *en,* and feminine plurals adding -*nen* to the singular ending -*in*.

A regular verb and the commonest numerals and days of the week are shown in tables before the main 100 units. Though verbs appear only in their infinitive form, their position in the units has been calculated from the total occurrence of all their parts.

Many German words may be translated by a number of English equivalents. Since it is assumed that the student will have access to a standard grammar and a standard dictionary, only the commonest equivalents have been cited; the work is designed not to clog the memory by listing all equivalents possible, but to stimulate interest by ensuring rapid, easy progress. When consulting the two indexes, the reader who cannot find a given word should try to think of synonyms or near-synonyms if certain words appear to be omitted.

The Indexes

The two indexes permit the student to use *German Key Words* as a first dictionary, but let it be repeated that the best available dictionary should be purchased to use in conjunction with the present aid if it is intended to continue with German past the elementary stage. The best possible grammar should be purchased too, by consulting your local international bookshop. *German Key Words* concentrates on standard written modern High German usage, from the mid-1960s to the mid-1990s.

Another fascinating use of the index is to discover how frequent – and consequently how relatively useful – each German word happens to be. Of course the frequency level applies only to the *German* words; nothing is implied at any point about the relative frequency of their English equivalents. Thus *Mark* appears in Unit 28 and *wiederhören* in Unit 61, though neither appears in a list of the commonest 2,000 words in English. Even the most casual observer may be curious to find that among the hundred most frequent words in German only two are nouns; if you care to guess which they are, you can check the answer, supplied at the end of this Introduction.

The first ten words are so common that they account for 34.79% of total occurrences in a lexical universe of nearly 1.8 million words; the first hundred account for 65.3% of total occurrences; and the first thousand for 83.2%, figures remarkably similar to word counts of French, Italian and Spanish by colleagues. It is therefore evident that anyone choosing to master the vocabulary set forth in *German Key Words* will need only another 17% or so to cover the entire lexical corpus encountered in books, magazines, newspapers, plays and films.

The Sources

The word-list draws on computer analysis of in excess of 1,775,000 words.

Sophisticated modern methods assist complex analysis, but it is clear from lateral comparison with word-lists from related languages that in general the 2,000 commonest words remain constant over a period of several decades, and to a lesser extent over centuries, because mankind's preoccupations remain essentially constant. The written word is more standard than the spoken word, and the majority of publications sampled avoid dialectal or slang usage.

Categories of literature sampled include but are not confined to the following: newspapers, periodicals in the fields of the arts, sciences and social sciences, general magazines issued weekly and monthly, novels and short stories, drama, poetry, works of biography, history and criticism, volumes of essays, religion and philosophy, but not highly technical monographs nor local newspapers.

The first conscientious attempt at a frequency dictionary in German was F.W. Kaeding's *Häufigkeitswörterbuch der deutschen Sprache* (Steglitz bei Berlin, 1897), but of course the age of that compilation renders it now of purely academic interest. Related publications of useable date include Georg Stötzel's 'Grunddeutsch' in *Linguistik und Didaktik* I (1970), pp. 195-204; 'Wortschatzvermittlung' by Wolfgang Dreibusch and Heidrun Zander in *International Review of Applied Linguistics in Language Teaching* IX (1971), pp. 131-145; Ulrich Engel's 'Bericht über das Forschungsunternehmen "Grundstrukturen der deutschen Sprache"' in *Sprache und Gesellschaft* (Jahrbuch 1970 des Instituts für deutsche Sprache, 1971, pp. 295-322); Robert Killinger's 'Die funktionale Gliederung des deutschen Wortschatzes' in *Germanistik* (1971), pp. 11-25; J. Alan Pfeffer's 'Grunddeutsch und die deutschen Entlehnungen aus fremden Sprachen' in *Wirkendes Wort* XXIIII (1973), and 'Grunddeutsch' in *Forschungsberichte des Instituts für deutschen Sprache* XXVII (1975); and Inger Rosengren's 'Der Grundwortschatz als theoretisches und praktisches Problem' in *Probleme der Lexikologie und Lexikographie* (Jahrbuch 1975 des Instituts für deutsche Sprache, 1976, pp. 313-333).

Newspaper German has been analysed in Inger Rosengren's *Ein Frequenzwörterbuch der deutschen Zeitungssprache* (2 vols., Lund, 1972-7), and fifteen years ago Heather Amory produced *The first thousand words in German* (London, 1979). The spoken language was dealt with in Arno Ruoff's *Häufigkeitswörterbuch gesprochener Sprache* (Tübingen, 1984-5), a book which divides German words into parts of speech: nouns, verbs, basic category (e.g. *sehr*), adjectives, adverbs, conjunctions, prepositions, particles, and articles. István Kosaras produced a German-German dictionary, *Grundwortschatz der deutschen Sprache* (Budapest and Berlin, 1980), consisting of 3,000 basic words but in alphabetical order rather than frequency order.

Great progress has been made in mechanolinguistics, permitting mechanical and electronic devices to scan ever larger samples of data; and in mathematical linguistics, allowing an ever more careful weighting of word usage.

I should like to acknowledge the great assistance offered by colleagues not only in the reunited Germany, Austria and Switzerland, but in Great Britain, Australia, the United States of America and Canada, and I thank also my dear wife Ortrud for help in the compilation of the German index, my editor Philip Ward for help in the compilation of the English index, and my friends at The Oleander Press who have collaborated so closely during the gestation of this book, which I trust will help a new generation of anglophone students keen to learn German.

September 1994   Dieter Zahn

N.B. The two nouns occurring in the commonest hundred German words are *Herr* and *Mann*.

Regular Verb
in the Present Tense
bauen, to build

ich baue I build

du baust you (*sg.*) build

er, sie, es baut he, she, it builds

wir bauen we build

Sie bauen you (*pl.*) build

sie bauen they build

Present Participle

bauend   building

Past Participle

gebaut   built

Regular Verb
in the Imperfect Tense

ich baute I built

du bautest you (*sg.*) built

er, sie, es baute he, she, it built

wir bauten we built

Sie bauten you (*pl.*) built

sie bauten they built

Cardinal Numerals

1 eins 2 zwei 3 drei 4 vier 5 fünf 6 sechs 7 sieben 8 acht 9 neun 10 zehn 11 elf 12 zwölf 13 dreizehn 20 zwanzig 21 einundzwanzig ... 30 dreissig 40 vierzig 50 fünfzig 60 sechzig 70 siebzig 80 achtzig 90 neunzig 100 hundert 1,000 tausend

Days of the Week

Sonntag Sunday Montag Monday Dienstag Tuesday Mittwoch Wednesday Donnerstag Thursday Freitag Friday Samstag Saturday

Unit 1

der (*m*.), die (*f*.), das (*n*.)   the

ein, eine, ein   a, an

von *prep*.   of, from

sein   to be

    ich bin I am   wir sind we are

    du bist you (*s*.) are   Sie sind you (*pl*.) are

    er, sie, es ist he, she, it is   sie sind they are

und *conj*.   and

haben   to have

    ich habe I have   wir haben we have

    du hast you (*s*.) have   Sie haben you (*pl*.) have

    er, sie, es hat he, she, it has   sie haben they have

zu *prep*.   to, too, at

er (*pl*. sie) *pron*.   he, it (*m*.), they

in *prep*.   in, into

sie (*pl*. sie) *pron*.   she, it (*f*.), they

es (*pl*. sie) *pron*.   it, they

ja *adv*.   yes

nicht *adv*.   not

daß *conj*.   that

dieser, diese, dieses *pron., adj*. this

Unit 2

werden — to be, become
- ich werde — wir werden
- du wirst — Sie werden
- er, sie, es wird — sie werden

aber *conj.* — but

auf *prep.* — on, upon

sein, seine, sein (*pl.* seine) *adj.* — one's, his, her, its

für *prep.* — for

kein, keine, kein (*pl.* keine) *adj.* — no, none

sich *pron.* — oneself, himself, herself, itself, themselves

jeder, jede, jedes (*pl.* jede) *pron., adj.* — each, every

oder *conj.* — or

man *pron.* — one (impersonal)

mit *prep.* — with

ich *pron.* — I

wie *adv.* — as, like, how

ab *prep.* — from
adv. — off

Unit 3

was *pron.*	what
machen	to make, do
Sie *pron.*	you (*pl.*)
sagen	to say
gut *adj.*	good
adv.	well
du *pron.*	you (*sg.*)
ihr *pron.*	you
adj.	her, its, their
tun	to do
mehr *adv.*	more
wo *adv.*	where
warum *adv.*	why
mein, meine, mein	my
(*pl.* meine) *pron., adj.*	
können	to be able to, can
wir *pron.*	we
ihrer, ihre, ihres *pron.*	hers, its, theirs
wohl *adv.*	well
Ihr *adj., pron.*	your

Unit 4

aus *prep.*	from
adv.	out
Ihrer, Ihre, Ihres *pron.*	your, yours
vor *prep.*	before
dein, deine, dein	your (*sg.*)
(*pl.* deine) *adj.*	
pron.	yours (*sg.*)
ganz *adj.*,	all, whole
adv.	quite, entirely
sehr *adv.*	very
viel *adj.*	much
wenn *conj.*	if
an *prep.*	at
adv.	on
wissen	to know
Herr *m.n.*	Mr, gentleman
stehen	to stand
noch *adv.*	still, yet
sehen	to see
unser, unsere, unser *adj.*	our
(*pl.* unsere) *pron.*	ours
sollen	to have to, ought to, should

Unit 5

Mann *m.n.*	man, husband
müssen	to have to, must
über *prep.*	above, over
als *conj.*	as, when, than
gross *adj.*	big, large, great, grand
auch *adv.*	also, too, even
kommen	to come
derselbe, dieselbe, dasselbe *pron., adj.*	same
bis *prep.*	till, up to
ohne *prep.*	without
wer *pron.*	who
gehen	to go
welcher, welche, welches *pron.*	which
einiger, einige, einiges *pron., adj.*	some, any
dürfen	to be allowed to, may
ja *adv.*	yes
stellen	to place, put
durch *prep.*	through

Unit 6

da *adv.*	then, there
conj.	because, since
bei *prep.*	with, at the house of
wann *adv.*	when
fort *adv.*	forwards, away, on
immer *adv.*	always, ever
wollen	to want, wish
um *prep.*	around, at (time)
nehmen	to take
nach *prep.*	after
denn *conj.*	for
so *adv.*	so
wenig *adj.*	little
adv.	slightly
nichts *pron.*	nothing
solcher, solche, solches *pron., adj.*	such, such a
finden	to find
klein *adj.*	small
also *conj.*	so, therefore
bezahlen	to pay
Stück *n.n.*	piece
Deutsch *n.n.*	German (language)

Unit 7

all (*pl.* alle)	all
glauben	to believe
doch *conj.*	but, nevertheless
adv.	indeed
seit *prep.*	since, for (time)
Uhr *f.n.*	clock, o'clock, watch
(*pl.* Uhren)	
nein *adv.*	no
eben *adj.*	even
adv.	just
dort *adv.*	there
geben	to give
nie(mals) *adv.*	never
antworten	to answer
Tag *m.n.*	day
Mal *n.n.*	time, mark, sign
nach *prep.*	after
unter *prep.*	below
nur *adv.*	only
schlecht *adj.*	bad
alles *pron.*	everything
legen	to place, put, lay
denn *conj.*	for

Unit 8

jener, jene, jenes *pron., adj.* (*pl.* jene)	that
weil *conj.*	because, since
nun *adv.*	now
interj.	well!
sprechen	to speak
Stunde *f.n.*	hour
schön *adj.*	beautiful, handsome, fine (danke schön, thanks very much)
ander *pron., adj.*	other
viel *adj.*	much (viele, many)
hier *adv.*	here
lassen	to let, leave
setzen	to put, place (sich setzen, to sit down)
damit *adv.*	by that
conj.	so that, with that
fahren	to go, travel
Frau *f.n.* (*pl.* Frauen)	woman, wife, Mrs
schon *adv.*	already, before
sicher *adj.*	safe, sure, certain
über *prep.*	above, over

Unit 9

wieviel *adj.*	how much (wieviele, how many)
bleiben	to remain
Leben *n.n.*	life
zwischen *prep.*	between
Zeit *f.n.* (*pl.* Zeiten)	time
natürlich *adj.*	natural
adv.	of course
während *prep.*	during
halten	to hold
erst *adj.*	first
adv.	at first
Ding *n.n.*	thing
dann *adv.*	then
scheinen	to seem, appear
kennen	to know (be acquainted with)
weder... noch ...*conj.*	neither ... nor ...
nachdem *conj.*	after
wegen *prep.*	because of
fragen	to ask
neu *adj.*	new
genug *adj.*	new
wiedersehen	to see again (Auf Wiedersehen!, Till we meet again!)

Unit 10

Welt *f.n.* (*pl.* Welten)	world
Moment *m.n.*	moment
n.n.	motive, factor
bestimmt *adj.*	certain
handeln	to act (handeln mit, to trade; handeln von, to deal with)
Auge *n.n.*	eye
ankommen	to arrive
entlang *prep.*	along
Jahr *n.n.*	year
jung	young
letzt *adj.*	last, latest
denken	to think
Haus (*pl.* Häuser) *n.n.*	house
gestatten	to permit
Kind (*pl.* Kinder)	child
Arbeit (*pl.* Arbeiten) *f.n.*	work
lieben	to love
Idee *f.n.*	idea
suchen	to seek, look for
endlich *adv.*	at last
wirklich *adv.*	really

Unit 11

danken	to thank
damit *adv.*	so that
je *adv.*	ever (je mehr, desto besser, the more, the better)
seitdem *conj.*	since
wohnen	to dwell, live (reside)
vielleicht *adv.*	perhaps, possibly
dafür *adv.*	for that
nötig *adj.*	necessary
Krieg *m.n.*	war
verstehen	to understand
möglich *adj.*	possible
her *adv.*	here
besser *adv.*	better
heute *adv.*	today
bevor *conj.*	before
Wort (*pl.* Wörter) *n.n.*	word
darauf *adv.*	on it, afterwards
jetzt *adv.*	now
gegen *prep.*	against
alt *adj.*	old

Unit 12

zurück *adv*.	back(wards)
daran *adv*.	at it, by it, on it
gegenüber *prep*.	opposite
kehren	to turn (sich kehren, to turn round)
Punkt *m.n.*	point
Frage *f.n.*	question
nah(e) *adj., adv.*	near
Nacht (*pl.* Nächte) *f.n.*	night
weit *adj.*	far, wide
Stadt (*pl.*Städte)	town, city
Name(n) *m.n.*	name
Freund *m.n.*	friend
folgen	to follow
Kopf (*pl.* Köpfe) *m.n.*	head
zeigen	to show
damals *adv.*	then
nämlich *adv.*	that is to say
selbst *pron.*	self
adv.	even
beinah(e) *adv.*	almost, nearly
leben	to live

Unit 13

obwohl *conj.*	although
Art (*pl.* Arten) *f.n.*	kind, sort, way
jawohl *adv.*	yes
wieder *adv.*	again, back
Morgen (*pl.* Morgen) *m.n.*	morning
sondern *conj.*	but (after negative)
Wasser (*pl.* Wasser) *n.n.*	water
dabei *adv.*	close (by)
bedeuten	to mean
Liebe *f.n.*	love
wider *prep.*	against, contrary to
lang *adj.*	long
darin *adv.*	in it
warten	to wait
oft *adv.*	often
beginnen	to begin
heissen	to be called
Ort *m.n.*	place
Null (*pl.* Nullen) *f.n.*	zero, nil
Abend *m.n.*	evening
bieten	to offer

Unit 14

tragen	to carry, bear
wahr *adj.*	true, real
Land (*pl.* Länder) *n.n.*	country, land, province
na! *interj.*	there!
Leute *pl.*	people
rechts *adv.*	on the right
Platz (*pl.* Plätze) *m.n.*	place, seat ,square
essen	to eat
bekommen	to get
Hand (*pl.* Hände) *f.n.*	hand
herein *adv.*	(in) here, inside
empfangen	to receive, conceive (a child)
Fall (*pl.* Fälle)	case, fall
nützen	to benefit
Teil *m.n. or n.n.*	part, share
Kraft (*pl.* Kräfte) *f.n.*	strength, force
allgemein *adj.*	general
Monat *m.n.*	month
erinnern	to remind (sich erinnern an, to remember)
Recht *n.n.*	right, law (recht haben, to be (in the) right

Unit 15

aufstehen	to get up
Seite *f.n.*	side, page
schmecken	to taste
Grund (*pl.*Gründe) *m.n.*	ground(s), base, basis
links *adv.*	on the left
deutsch *adj.*	German
falls *conj.*	if, in case
schlagen	to hit, strike
gern(e) *adv.*	gladly (gern haben, to like)
dagegen *adv.*	against it
spielen	to play
Sache *f.n.*	thing, fact
Gesellschaft *f.n.*	company, society
heraus *adv.*	(out) here, outside
Dame *f.n.*	lady
voll *adj.*	full
rufen	to call, shout
zuerst *adj.*	at first
schreiben	to write
Erde *f.n.*	earth, world
reisen	to travel

Unit 16

warum *adv.*	why
eintreten	to go in, enter
fern *adj.*	far, distant
rühren	to move
Film *m.n.*	film
bewegen	to move
ziemlich *adv.*	rather
Tür *(pl.* Türen) *f.n.*	gate, door
hinein *adv.*	(in) there
Geschäft *n.n.*	business, deal
Beispiel *n.n.*	example (zum Beispiel, for example)
nennen	to call, name
ansehen	to look at, consider
weiss *adj.*	white
hinaus *adv.*	out there
innen *adv.*	within
Mädchen (*pl.* Mädchen) *n.n.*	girl
lernen	to learn
Zimmer (*pl.* Zimmer) *n.n.*	room
Vater (*pl.* Väter) *m.n.*	father
ausser *adv.*	besides
prep.	out of, outside, apart from

Unit 17

her *adv.*	here, since (schon langer her, a long time ago)
Körper (*pl.* Körper) *m.n.*	body
leicht *adj.*	simple, light, easy
Sohn (*pl.* Söhne) *m.n.*	son
trotz *prep.*	in spite of
Sport *m.n.*	sport
Jugend *f.n.*	youth
erkennen	to recognise
arbeiten	to work
Tochter (*pl.* Töchter) *f.n.*	daughter
Fernsehen *n.n.*	television
glücklich *adj.*	happy, lucky
schlimm *adj.*	bad, evil
oben *adv.*	above
Kunst (*pl.* Künste) *f.n.*	art
schenken	to give, present
Resultat *n.n.*	result
Ruhe *f.n.*	rest
Zweifel (*pl.*Zweifel) *m.n.*	doubt
Mitte *f.n.*	middle

Unit 18

früh *adj.*	early
Nummer (*pl.* Nummern) *f.n.*	number
lesen	to read
Restaurant (*pl.* Restaurants) *n.n.*	restaurant
öffnen	to open
unten *adv.*	underneath
Radio (*pl.* Radios) *n.n.*	radio
kurz *adj.*	short
vorder *adj.*	fore(most), front
Ende *n.n.*	end
hoch *adj.*	high
anhalten	to stop
Büro (*pl.* Büros) *n.n.*	office
fühlen	to touch, feel
Staat *m.n.*	state
längs *prep.*	along
fortsetzen	to continue
Mittag *m.n.*	midday
ziehen	to pull, draw
tatsächlich *adv.*	actually
reichen	to reach

Unit 19

gerade *adj.*	straight
adv.	directly
steigen	to rise, climb
vorig *adj.*	previous
reden	to speak, talk
mehrere *adj.*	several
vergessen	to forget
erholen	to recover (sich erholen, to recover, get better
Gott (*pl.* Götter) *m.n.*	god, God
fallen	to fall
genügen	to suffice
stecken	to put, place
gewiss *adj.*	certain, sure
Rechnung *f.n.*	invoice, bill
Mensch (*pl.*Menschen) *m.n.*	human being
genau *adj., adv.*	exact, exactly
stark *adj.*	strong
Buch (*pl.* Bücher) *n.n.*	book
Mittel (*pl.* Mittel) *n.n.*	means
frei *adj.*	free
Meister (*pl.* Meister) *m.n.*	master
einmal *adv.*	once

Unit 20

sogar *adv.*	even
verlieren	to lose
etwas *adj.*	a little, some
adv.	quite, rather
pron.	anything, something
schwarz *adj.*	black
wünschen	to want, wish
dazu *adv.*	to it
angenehm *adj.*	agreeable, pleasant
lieb *adj.*	dear
bringen	to bring
Jahrhundert *n.n.*	century
dienen	to serve
darum *adv.*	around it
jemand *pron.*	anyone, someone
schiessen	to shoot
Sicht *f.n.*	sight
Nachmittag *m.n.*	afternoon
Luft (*pl.* Lüfte) *m.n.*	air
spät *adj.*	late
treffen	to meet
los *adj.*	free, loose
adv.	away (los! away you go!)
Mutter (*pl.* Mütter) *f.n.*	mother

Unit 21

anfangen	to begin
gefallen	to please (es gefällt mir, I like it)
danach *adv.*	after it
Person (*pl.* Personen) *f.n.*	person
dick *adj.*	thick, fat
Herz (*pl.* Herzen) *n.n.*	nation, people
entwickeln	to develop
Volk (*pl.* Völker) *n.n.*	nation, people
rein *adj.*	clean, pure
sterben	to die
daraus *adv.*	from it
Stimme *f.n.*	voice
bös(e) *adj.*	bad, evil
Fuss (*pl.*Füsse) *m.n.*	foot
daher *adv.*	from there
Partei (*pl.* Parteien) *f.n.*	(political) party
Schlag (*pl.* Schläge) *m.n.*	blow
Strasse *f.n.*	road, street
verboten *adj.*	forbidden
sichern	to protect, secure
statt *prep.*	instead of

Unit 22

abfahren	to depart
Geld (*pl.* Gelder) *n.n.*	money
erhalten	to obtain
besetzen	to occupy
träumen	to dream
Mitte *f.n.*	middle
best *adj.*	best (*adv.* am besten, best)
Sonne *f.n.*	sun
teuer *adj.*	dear (of price)
Ordnung *f.n.*	order
Weg *m.n.*	route, way
existieren	to exist
Wert *m.n.*	value, worth
Republik (*pl.* Republiken) *f.n.*	republic
beide *adj., pron.*	both
begegnen	to meet
Tod *m.n.*	death
herkommen	to come (here)
Weise *f.n.*	manner, way
ändern	to alter, change
überall *adv.*	everywhere

Unit 23

bitten	to ask, request
Gegenständ (*pl.* Gegenstände) *m.n.*	object
morgen *adv.*	tomorrow
zahlreich *adj.*	numerous
gelegentlich *adj.*	occasional
zusammen *adv.*	together
Fach (*pl.* Fächer) *n.n.*	subject, compartment
Bewegung *f.n.*	movement
Achtung! *interj.*	Attention!
rund *adj.*	round
jedoch *adv.*	however, yet
Tisch *m.n.*	table
Problem *n.n.*	problem
darüber *adv.*	over it
geschehen	to happen
Gestalt (*pl.* Gestalten) *f.n.*	form, shape
hinter *prep.*	behind
verhindern	to prevent
besprechen	to discuss
ober *adj.*	higher, upper
herauf *adv.*	(up) here

Unit 24

davon *adv.*	from it, of it
Spiel *n.n.*	game
soviel *conj.*	as far as
adv.	as much, so much
menschlich *adj.*	human
Linie *f.n.*	line
irgendein *adj.*	any, some
behalten	to keep
unmöglich *adj.*	impossible
Eingang *m.n.*	entrance
Gesicht (*pl.* Gesichter) *n.n.*	face
dadurch *adv.*	through it
gelten	to cost, be worth
Dienst *f.n.*	service
erscheinen	to appear
neben *prep.*	near
wechseln	to (ex)change
Vergnügen *n.n.*	enjoyment, pleasure
(*pl.* Vergnügen)	
hinab *adv.*	from there
Familie *f.n.*	family
Seele *f.n.*	soul, spirit
gar nicht	not at all

Unit 25

anders *adj.*	different
fast *adv.*	almost, nearly
fordern	to demand
herum *adv.*	(a)round, about
Erinnerung *f.n.*	memory
verlassen	to vacate, leave
fehlen	to lack, be missing
Himmel (*pl.* Himmel) *m.n.*	heaven, sky
aussehen	to appear, look
zumachen	to close
zweit *adj.*	second
besitzen	to possess
arm *adj.*	poor
Zeitung *f.n.*	newspaper
Feuer (*pl.* Feuer) *n.n.*	fire
Zentrum (*pl.* Zentren) *n.n.*	centre
Spass (*pl.* Spässe) *m.n.*	fun (Viel Spass! Have fun!)
entdecken	to discover
leisten	to do, accomplish
fremd *adj.*	foreign, strange
Licht (*pl.* Lichter) *n.n.*	light

Unit 26

Bundesrepublik *f.n.*   Federal Republic

fertig *adj.*   ready

treiben   to drive, move

dahin *adv.*   over there

breit *adj.*   broad

darstellen   to represent

Zahl (*pl.* Zahlen) *f.n.*   number

aussen *adv.*   outside

Fehler (*pl.* Fehler) *m.n.*   error

vorher *adv.*   beforehand

Gegenteil *m.n.*   contrary (im Gegenteil, on the contrary

zuhören   to listen

gleich *adj.*   the same, equal

laufen   to run, walk

Mark (*pl.* Mark) *f.n.*   mark (unit of currency) (*pl.* Marken, boundaries)

anmachen   to turn on

Rad (*pl.* Räder) *n.n.*   wheel

Politik *f.n.*   politics

übrigens *adv.*   by the way

versuchen   to attempt, try

eigentlich *adj.*   actual, real

    adv.   actually, really

Unit 27

Woche *f.n.*	week
hinten *adv.*	behind
Preis *m.n.*	price
etwa *adv.*	about
Mass *n.n.*	measure
Zustand (*pl.* Zustände) *m.n.*	state
regieren	to govern
addieren	to add
Lage *f.n.*	situation, position
heran *adv.*	near, up to
Natur *f.n.*	nature
Kost *f.n.*	food (*pl.* Kosten, costs)
führen	to lead
Saal (*pl.* Säle) *m.n.*	hall, (large) room
meinen	to mean, think
nachher *adv.*	afterwards
vollkommen *adj.*	finished, perfect
wichtig *adj.*	important
darein *adv.*	into it
Eintritt *m.n.*	entrance
Speise *f.n.*	food

Unit 28

ausmachen	to turn off
Geschichte *f.n.*	history
hinunter *adv.*	downwards
werfen	to throw
annehmen	to accept
Gebiet *n.n.*	area, region
Anschein *m.n.*	appearance
wert *adj.*	worth
Schritt *m.n.*	step
aufwärts *adv.*	upwards
drücken	to press, push
Augenblick *m.n.*	instant, moment
zahlen	to pay
gestern *adv.*	yesterday
herab *adv.*	downwards
Regierung *f.n.*	government
Laden (*pl.* Läden) *m.n.*	shop
völlig *adj.*	complete, whole
adv.	completely, wholly
hören	to hear
vorhin *adv.*	a short while ago
speisen	to dine, eat

Unit 29

Ausgang (*pl.* Ausgänge) *m.n.*	exit
Hotel (*pl.* Hotels) *n.n.*	hotel
tief *adj.*	deep, profound
Herkunft *f.n.*	birth, origin
abwärts *adv.*	downwards
besteigen	to climb, ascent
vollenden	to complete, finish
darunter *adv.*	under it
herstellen	to produce
woanders *adv.*	somewhere else
heben	to raise
Minute *f.n.*	minute
Student (*pl.* Studenten) *m.n.* Studentin *f.n.*	student
damals *adv.*	then
verschieden *adj.*	different
beilegen	to add
Reise *f.n.*	journey
Schule *f.n.*	school
rechnen	to calculate
allerdings *adv.*	certainly
hübsch *adj.*	pretty, nice

Unit 30

Güte *f.n.*	goodness
hin *adv.*	there, towards, (hin und her, to and fro)
schlafen	to sleep
Mühe *f.n.*	trouble, pain
zurückhalten	to hold back
Ach! *interj.*	Oh! Hey!
Schwierigkeit *f.n.*	difficulty
König *m.n.*	king
Richtung *f.n.*	direction
begreifen	to perceive
Blume *f.n.*	flower
schnell *adj., adv.*	quick(ly)
Wahrheit *f.n.*	truth
Klasse *f.n.*	class
abends *adv.*	in the evening
einmal *adv.*	once
woran *adv.*	about what, on which
rennen	to run
privat *adv.*	private
herbei *adv.*	here, this way
einfach *adj.*	simple

Unit 31

mitten *adv.*	in the middle
Farbe *f.n.*	colour
aufheben	to lift, raise
daneben *adv.*	near it
früher *adj.*	earlier
adv.	earlier on
kurz *adj.*	short
halb *adj.*	half
Not (*pl.* Nöte) *f.n.*	need, shortage
Schuld (*pl.* Schulden) *f.n.*	debt, guilt
verkaufen	to sell
Junge *m.n.*	boy
bemerken	to remark
niedrig *adj.*	low
hervor *adv.*	forth
See *f.n.*	sea
m.n.	lake
Wirklichkeit *f.n.*	reality
politisch *adj.*	political
dauern	to last
Dasein *n.n.*	existence
hinauf *adv.*	upwards
ausdrücken	to express

Unit 32

bilden	to educate, form
Auto (*pl.* Autos) *n.n.*	car
hell *adj.*	bright, light
Wissenschaft *f.n.*	knowledge, science
schieben	to push
brechen	to break
womit *adv.*	with which
urteilen	to judge
verzeihen	to pardon
bald *adv.*	soon
wiederholen	to repeat
reich *adj.*	rich
Brief *m.n.*	letter
dunkel *adj.*	dark
hart *adj.*	hard, rough
Wind *m.n.*	wind
hinüber *adv.*	over there
süss *adj.*	sweet
Friede(n) (*pl.* Frieden) *m.n.*	peace
Dank *m.n.*	thanks
Karte *f.n.*	card, map, ticket

Unit 33

bitte *interj.*	please
klar *adj.*	clear
befördern	to convey
gemein *adj.*	common
lieber *adj.*	dearer
adv.	rather (lieber haben, to prefer)
hoffen	to hope
ablehnen	to refuse
vertreten	to represent
riesig *adj.*	huge
Ehre *f.n.*	honour
entschuldigen	to excuse
drehen	to turn
bloss *adj.*	mere, simple
adv.	merely, simply
Kaffee (*pl.* Kaffees) *m.n.*	coffee
Schluss (*pl.* Schlüsse) *m.n.*	end
Herrin *f.n.*	lady
herzu *adv.*	(to) here
Bild (*pl.* Bilder) *n.n.*	picture
Knabe *m.n.*	boy
überlegen *adj.*	superior
Ergebnis *n.n.* (*pl.* Ergebnisse)	result

Unit 34

Fräulein (*pl.* Fräulein) *n.n.*	Miss
Kirche *f.n.*	church
billig *adj.*	cheap
fördern	to promote
Wald (*pl.* Wälder) *m.n.*	forest, wood
Bruder *m.n.*	brother
gebären	to bear (geboren, born)
Heilige(r) *f.n.*, *m.n.*	saint
schulden	to owe
leiten	to lead
Rand (*pl.* Ränder) *m.n.*	edge
Blick *n.n.*	glance, look
Wetter *n.n.*	weather
kaufen	to buy
Rolle *f.n.*	rôle, roll
aussteigen	to alight, descend
Getränk *n.n.*	drink
Macht (*pl.* Mächte) *f.n.*	power
Feld (*pl.* Felder) *n.n.*	field
dahinter *adv.*	over there
weniger *adj.*	less(er)

Unit 35

Freude *f.n.*	delight, joy
erklären	to declare, explain
Kleid (*pl.* Kleider) *n.n.*	dress, clothes
aufhören	to cease, stop
anderswo *adv.*	elsewhere
ankündigen	to announce
Geschmack (*pl.* Geschmäcke) *m.n.*	taste
dritt *adj.*	third
Haupt (*pl.* Häupter) *n.n.*	chief, head, leader (Haupt-, main, principal)
Periode *f.n.*	period
Nutzen (*pl.* Nutzen) *m.n.*	advantage, use
Armee *f.n.*	army
echt *adj.*	genuine, real
herüber *adv.*	across here
Musik *f.n.*	music
Silber *n.n.*	silver
beendigen	to end
Kerl *m.n.*	fellow
rot *adj.*	red
erzählen	to narrate, tell
Stuhl (*pl.* Stühle) *m.n.*	chair

Unit 36

grün *adj.*	green
Abfahrt *m.n.*	departure
laut *adj.*	loud
adv.	aloud
prep.	according to
vorbereiten	to prepare
gehören	to belong
Artikel (*pl.* Artikel) *m.n.*	article
unwissend *adj.*	ignorant
Hund *m.n.*	dog
bewahren	to preserve
Handel *m.n.*	commerce, trade
interessant *adj.*	interesting
sanft *adj.*	gentle, soft
mögen *f.n.*	to like
Autorität *f.n.*	authority
Beruf *m.n.*	job, profession
Ehe *f.n.*	marriage
allzu *adv.*	all too, much too
gering *adj.*	small, insignificant
Eltern *pl.*	parents
Eindruck (*pl.* Eindrücke) *m.n.*	impression
Gold *n.n.*	gold

Unit 37

kriegen	to get
Fahrt (*pl.* Fahrten) *f.n.*	journey, trip
schicken	to send
behandeln	to treat, handle
schwer *adj.*	difficult, heavy, hard
Freiheit *f.n.*	freedom, liberty
hoffentlich *adv.*	hopefully
gelangen	to attain, reach
nützlich *adj.*	useful
Anhalt *m.n.*	stop, support
Vorfall (*pl.* Vorfälle) *m.n.*	event, incident
Rückkehr *f.n.*	return
Angst (*pl.* Ängste) *f.n.*	fear
Wichtigkeit *f.n.*	importance
empor *adv.*	upwards
Aussehen *m.n.*	appearance
zurückkommen	to come back, return
Rest *m.n.*	remainder
einschliessen	to include
grüssen	to greet
Denken *n.n.*	thought

Unit 38

Anfang (*pl.* Anfänge) *m.n.*	start
ersetzen	to replace
gewöhnlich *adj.*	ordinary, usual
schaffen	to create
Pferd *n.n.*	horse
selbstverständlich *adv.*	naturally, of course
Deutschland *n.n.*	Germany
ökonomisch *adj.*	economic
lebendig *adj.*	living
Bericht *m.n.*	report, account
verlangen	to demand, require
blau *adj.*	blue
Firma (*pl.* Firmen) *f.n.*	firm, company
vertrauen	to confide
vollständig *adj.*	complete
mitkommen	to come (along) with
Baum (*pl.* Bäume) *m.n.*	tree
Gruppe *f.n.*	group
kalt *adj.*	cold
schlimm *adj.*	bad, evil
entscheiden	to decide
sorgen (für)	to take care (of)

Unit 39

brauchen	to need, require
Tee *m.n.*	tea
betreffen	to concern
Gruss (*pl.* Grüsse) *m.n.*	greeting
waschen	to wash
Arm *m.n.*	arm
Wand (*pl.* Wände) *f.n.*	wall
zählen	to count
wunderbar *adj.*	marvellous
auferlegen	to impose
gewöhnen	to accustom
bewachen	to guard
senden	to send
streng *adj., adv.*	severe(ly), stern(ly)
trinken	to drink
Übereinstimmung *f.n.*	agreement
Interesse *n.n.*	interest
Schiff *n.n.*	ship
Grundsatz (*pl.* Grundsätze) *m.n.*	principle
zurückgehen	to go back, return
verwirklichen	to realise (sich verwirklichen, to come true)

Unit 40

niemand	nobody
ebenso *adv.*	equally, just so
unterscheiden	to distinguish
Erfolg *m.n.*	success
untersuchen	to examine
anwesend *adj.*	present
solang(e) *conj.*	as long as
ungewöhnlich *adj.*	unusual
allerlei *adj.*	all sorts of
Szene *f.n.*	scene
Verkauf *m.n.*	sale
eilig *adj.*	fast
Gewohnheit *f.n.*	custom, habit
beobachten	to observe
Winter (*pl.* Winter) *m.n.*	winter
relativ *adj.*	relative
Behörde *f.n.*	authority
übereinstimmen	to agree
offen *adj.*	open
Verwandte(r) *f.n., m.n.*	relation
Nähe *f.n.*	vicinity (in der Nähe von, *adv.,* close to)

Unit 41

Wesen *n.n.*	being, substance
Rundgang *m.n.* (*pl.* Rundgänge)	tour
verfolgen	to pursue
zuletzt *adv.*	at last
Regen *m.n.*	rain
interessieren	to interest (sich interessieren für, to be interested in)
Vertrauen *n.n.*	confidence, trust
deuten	to explain
Sommer (*pl.* Sommer) *m.n.*	summer
offenbaren	to reveal
nutzlos *adj.*	useless
Dorf (*pl.*Dörfer) *n.n.*	village
Betrag (*pl.* Beträge) *m.n.*	amount, sum
allein *adj.*	assisted
adv.	alone
conj.	yet, but
recht *adj.*	right
Minister (*pl.* Minister) *m.n.*	minister
ergreifen	to seize
Figur (*pl.* Figuren)	figure
aktuell *adj.*	contemporary, current
Regime *m.n.*	regime
ungefähr *adv.*	about

Unit 42

Doktor (*pl.* Doktoren) *m.n.*	doctor
Programm *n.n.*	program(me)
öffentlich *adj.*	public
Titel (*pl.* Titel) *m.n.*	title
Verzeihung *f.n.*	pardon (Verzeihung! Excuse me!)
Schatz (*pl.* Schätze) *m.n.*	darling, treasure
manchmal *adv.*	sometimes
Vogel (*pl.* Vögel) *m.n.*	bird
fest *adj.*	firm, secure
gründen	to establish, found
Arbeiter (*pl.* Arbeiter) *m.n.*	worker
hereinlassen	to admit
Strom (*pl.* Ströme) *m.n.*	current, river, stream
mild *adj.*	mild
Bundestag *m.n.*	German Parliament
System *n.n.*	system
Schüler (*pl.* Schüler) *m.n.* (Schülerin, *f.n.*)	pupil
Antwort (*pl.* Antworten) *f.n.*	answer
verteidigen	to defend
zweifeln	to doubt
Künstler (*pl.* Künstler) *m.n.* (Künstlerin *f.n.*)	artist

Unit 43

Schweigen *n.n.*	silence
anstellen	to employ
Wunsch (*pl.* Wünsche) *m.n.*	wish
lachen	to laugh
Verstand (*pl.* Verstände) *m.n.*	understanding
bestehen	to be, exist (bestehen auf, to insist on; bestehen aus, to consist of)
sobald *adv.*	as soon as
Zeichen (*pl.* Zeichen) *n.n.*	sign
putzen	to clean
fein *adj.*	fine
Qualität (*pl.* Qualitäten) *f.n.*	quality
Sorge *f.n.*	care, worry
Punkt *m.n.*	point
Dichter *m.n.*	poet
weg *adv.*	away
Tier *n.n.*	animal
erfolgreich *adj.*	successful
Raum (*pl.* Räume) *m.n.*	space, room
enthalten	to contain
verschwinden	to disappear
Vertreter (*pl.* Vertreter) *m.n.* (Vertreterin *f.n.*)	representative

Unit 44

inner *adj.*	inner, internal
Gelegenheit *f.n.*	occasion, opportunity
französisch *adj.*	French
mittlerweile *adv.*	meanwhile
Zukunft *f.n.*	future
mitbringen	to bring along
Fabrik (*pl.* Fabriken) *f.n.*	factory
marschieren	to march
Schrei (*pl.* Schreie) *m.n.*	cry, shout
kreuzen	to cross, pass through
fähig *adj.*	capable
entkommen	to escape
Schlaf *m.n.*	sleep
abwesend *adj.*	absent
feststellen	to ascertain
verbinden	to connect, join
pflegen	to care for
vermieten	to let, rent out
Arzt (*pl.* Ärzte) *m.n.*	doctor (medical)
Stein *m.n.*	stone
link *adj.*	left

Unit 45

passen	to fit, suit
gegenwärtig *adj.*	present
befassen	to concern
Inhalt *m.n.*	content(s)
heiss *adj.*	hot
Papier *n.n.*	paper
gewinnen	to win
Stoff *m.n.*	material, matter
bereit *adj.*	ready
Glas (*pl.* Gläser) *n.n.*	glass
berühmt *adj.*	famous
viereckig *adj.*	square
erstaunen	to astonish
behandeln	to handle, treat
Wagen (*pl.* Wagen) *m.n.*	car, cart, coach
Soldat (*pl.* Soldaten) *m.n.*	soldier
Berg *m.n.*	mountain
Schloss (*pl.* Schlösser) *n.n.*	castle
nächst *adj.*	nearest, next
vorschlagen	to propose, suggest

Unit 46

eingehen	to enter
Stern *m.n.*	star
entzückend *adj.*	charming
absteigen	to descend
schreien	to cry, shout
europäisch *adj.*	European
Glück *n.n.*	happiness, luck
Wille(n) *m.n.*	will
sauber *adj.*	clean
richtig *adj.*	right
Bett (*pl.* Betten) *n.n.*	bed
ungeheuer *adj.*	enormous, huge
vorbei *adv.*	past
festmachen	to fasten
Quantität (*pl.* Quantitäten) *f.n.*	quantity
berichtigen	to correct
widersprechen	to contradict
vormittags *adv.*	in the morning
schweigen	to be silent
amerikanisch *adj.*	American

Unit 47

Traum (*pl.* Träume) *m.n.*	dream
weiter *adj.*	wider
adv.	farther, further (und so weiter, and so on)
Mitglied (*pl.* Mitglieder) *n.n.*	member
sofort *adv.*	immediately
Einkauf (*pl.* Einkäufe) *m.n.*	purchase
Publikum *n.n.*	public
einkommen	to come in, enter
Blitz *m.n.*	flash, lightning
Wein *m.n.*	wine
beziehen	to cover
Probe *f.n.*	proof, test
mieten	to rent
Landschaft *f.n.*	countryside
folgend *adj.*	following
behaupten	to maintain, state
zufällig *adj.*	accidental
adv.	by chance
ausgezeichnet *adj.*	excellent
einzig *adj.*	only, sole
traurig *adj.*	sad
Gesetz *n.n.*	law

Unit 48

überhaupt *adv.*	in general
anreden	to address, speak to
Vergangenheit *f.n.*	past
Theater (*pl.* Theater) *n.n.*	theatre
Markt (*pl.* Markte) *m.n.*	market
Verhalten *n.n.*	behaviour
aufrichten	to erect, set up
singen	to sing
ähnlich *adj.*	similar
Schnee *m.n.*	snow
aussprechen	to pronounce
Eisen (*pl.* Eisen) *n.n.*	iron
besonders *adv.*	particularly, (e)specially
moralisch *adj.*	moral
Gerechtigkeit *f.n.*	justice
Arbeitgeber *m.n.* (*pl.* Arbeitgeber)	employer
Gatte *m.n.* (Gattin *f.n.*)	spouse, husband, (wife)
eingehend *adj.*	thorough
lächeln	to smile
hinan *adv.*	up to
schliessen	to close

Unit 49

Gegenwart *f.n.*	present (time)
Fleisch *n.n.*	meat
anwenden	to apply
stützen	to support
Prüfung *f.n.*	examination
aufsteigen	to climb up
Durchfahrt (*pl.* Durchfahrten) *f.n.*	passage
Nord(en) *m.n.*	north
Gewissen *n.n.*	conscience
glänzend *adj.*	brilliant
Hochzeit *f.n.*	marriage, wedding
Feind *m.n.*	enemy
sicherlich *adv.*	surely
direkt *adj.*	direct, straight
falsch *adj.*	false
Sorte *f.n.*	kind, sort
Stelle *f.n.*	place
Einzelheit *f.n.*	detail
klug *adj.*	clever
Umstand (*pl.* Umstände) *m.n.*	circumstance

Unit 50

Garten (*pl.* Gärten) *m.n.*	garden
Ziel *n.n.*	aim, goal
nachfolgen	to succeed
Glaube *m.n.*	belief, faith
Gedanke *m.n.*	thought
Flugzeug *n.n.*	aeroplane, aircraft
Quelle *f.n.*	origin, source, spring
studieren	to study
nachdenken	to ponder
ob *conj.*	whether (als ob, as if)
retten	to save, preserve
Sorgfalt *f.n.*	care, worry
wählen	to choose, select
Position *f.n.*	position
bezeichnen	to designate, mark
Aufgabe *f.n.*	duty, exercise (homework)
schwach *adj.*	feeble, weak
begehren	to desire
wagen	to dare
Erscheinen *n.n.*	appearance

Unit 51

krank *adj.*	ill
Präsident (*pl.* Präsidenten) *m.n.*	President
Lehrer (*pl.* Lehrer) *m.n.* (Lehrerin, *f.n.*)	teacher
gesellig *adj.*	social
Abenteuer (*pl.* Abenteuer) *n.n.*	adventure
modern *adj.*	modern
Bereich *n.n.*	domain, field
einsteigen	to get in
Kenntnis (*pl.* Kenntnisse) *f.n.*	knowledge
national *adj.*	national
Tafel (*pl.* Tafeln) *f.n.*	board, table
zart *adj.*	delicate, gentle
prüfen	to prove, test
Methode *f.n.*	method
hauptsächlich *adv.*	principally
vermeiden	to avoid
Fenster (*pl.* Fenster) *n.n.*	window
strecken	to stretch
dirigieren	to direct
prächtig *adj.*	magnificent

Unit 52

leider *adv.*	unfortunately
Besitz *m.n.*	possession
Gewissheit *f.n.*	certainty
vergrössern	to enlarge
begleiten	to accompany
Zeugnis (*pl.* Zeugnisse) *n.n.*	testimony
Leidenschaft *f.n.*	passion
verdienen	to deserve, earn
tot *adj.*	dead
anerkennen	to acknowledge
Geheimnis (*pl.* Geheimnisse) *n.n.*	secret
umher *adv.*	hereabouts
null *adj.*	null, zero
wohltun	to do good
Schnitt *m.n.*	cut
wovon *adv.*	from which, of which
Süd(en) *m.n.*	south
weh *adj.*	sad, sore (weh tun, to hurt)
interj.	alas!
tätig *adj.*	active, employed
kennenlernen	to become acquainted

Unit 53

Überraschung *f.n.*	surprise
voran *adv.*	in front
seltsam *adj.*	curious, strange
fürchten	to fear
Hoffnung *f.n.*	hope
Schwester (*pl.* Schwestern) *f.n.*	sister
geschlossen *adj.*	closed
Mund (*pl.* Munder) *m.n.*	mouth
äusser *adj.*	external, outer
Viertel (*pl.* Viertel) *n.n.*	district, quarter
Zeuge *m.n.*	witness
Krankheit *f.n.*	illness, disease
abbrechen	to break off
Wahl (*pl.* Wahlen) *f.n.*	choice, electrion
nackt *adj.*	bare, naked
gewähren	to allow, grant
zahllos *adj.*	numerous
Element *n.n.*	element
töten	to kill
Vorschlag (*pl.* Vorschläge) *m.n.*	suggestion

Unit 54

Frühling *m.n.*	spring
weinen	to weep
Provinz (*pl.* Provinzen) *f.n.*	province
befestigen	to fix
Orden (*pl.* Orden) *m.n.*	order
Neid *m.n.*	envy
Kommerz *m.n.*	commerce
greifen	to grasp, seize
selten *adj.*	rare
adv.	rarely
erregen	to excite
Hochachtung *f.n.*	regard, respect
Hunger *m.n.*	hunger
voraus *adv.*	ahead
näher *adj.*	closer
Halt *m.n.*	stop, support
wozu *adv.*	to which
vornehm *adj.*	distinguished
ausserordentlich *adj.*	extraordinary
Ost(en) *m.n.*	east
gesund *adj.*	healthy, well
Verfasser (*pl.* Verfasser) *m.n.*	author

Unit 55

verstecken	to hide
Eile *f.n.*	haste, hurry
bedauern	to regret, be sorry for
Innere *n.n.*	interior
ausruhen (sich)	to (have a) rest
Meinung *f.n.*	opinion
lärmen	to make a noise
Kino (*pl.* Kinos) *n.n.*	cinema
Ausnahme *f.n.*	exception
einander *pron.*	each other, one another
vorhergehend *adj.*	preceding
Lesen *n.n.*	reading
vermindern	to reduce
West(en) *m.n.*	west
unterhalten	to converse, keep (sich unterhalten, to enjoy oneself)
Nachricht (*pl.* Nachrichten) *f.n.*	report, *pl.* news
vereinbar *adj.*	compatible, consistent
Frist (*pl.* Fristen) *f.n.*	period, term
Palast (*pl.* Paläste) *m.n.*	palace
überraschen	to surprise
Leid (*pl.* Leiden) *n.n.*	grief, sorrow

Unit 56

geöffnet *adj.*	open
Einheit *f.n.*	unit, unity
Boot *n.n.*	boat
verpflichten (sich)	to commit (oneself)
geheim *adj.*	secret
schrecklich *adj.*	terrible
voraussagen	to foresee
Stellung *f.n.*	position
gewissenhaft *adj.*	conscientious
verloren *adj.*	lost
Ankunft (*pl.* Ankünfte) *f.n.*	arrival
Verein *m.n.*	association, society
Unterhalt *m.n.*	keep, support
frisch *adj.*	fresh, lively
Café (*pl.* Cafés) *n.n.*	café
ausnehmen	to exclude, take out
Misserfolg *m.n.*	failure
insbesondere *adv.*	especially
nimmer *adv.*	never
Vormittag *m.n.*	morning

Unit 57

Tätigkeit *f.n.*	activity
anzeigen	to indicate
Blut *n.n.*	blood
Plan (*pl.* Pläne) *m.n.*	intention, plan
überholen	to overtake
persönlich *adj.*	personal
verrückt *adj.*	crazy, mad
Stirn *f.n.*	forehead
Versuch *m.n.*	attempt
plötzlich *adj.*	sudden
adv.	suddenly
wobei *adv.*	whereby
Eigenschaft *f.n.*	quality
Weh *n.n.*	pain
vorerst *adv.*	for the time being
aufgeben	to give up
Entschuldigung *f.n.*	excuse
Viereck *n.n.*	square
beschäftigt *adj.*	busy
Krise *f.n.*	crisis
Geographie *f.n.*	geography

Unit 58

später *adj.*	later
Agent (*pl.* Agenten) *m.n.*	agent
General *m.n.*	general
besuchen	to visit
Jugend *f.n.*	youth
liefern	to supply
präzis *adj.*	precise
Elend *n.n.*	misery
Eck *n.n.*	corner
leid *adj.*	disagreeable (es tut mir leid, I'm sorry)
Professor (*pl.* Professoren) *m.n.*	professor
trocken *adj.*	dry
Lärm *m.n.*	noise
entgehen	to escape
Unterhaltung *f.n.*	amusement, conversation
kühl *adj.*	cool
Zahn (*pl.* Zähne) *m.n.*	tooth
wiederkehren	to return
erregt *adj.*	excited
Druck (*pl.* Drücke) *m.n.*	impression, print

Unit 59

bewohnen	to inhabit
Gesundheit *f.n.*	health
Brot *n.n.*	bread
sonst *adv.*	otherwise
trennen (sich)	to separate
gerecht *adj.*	just
adv.	justly
Boden (*pl.* Böden) *m.n.*	floor, ground
erleben	to undergo
sonderbar *adj.*	strange
Schicksal *n.n.*	destiny, fate
Änderung *f.n.*	change
Gunst *f.n.*	favour
Schönheit *f.n.*	beauty
nähern (sich)	to approach
Stock (*pl.* Stöcke) *m.n.*	stock, storey
ausbrechen	to break out
Pflicht (*pl.* Pflichten) *f.n.*	duty
wiederbringen	to bring back
Vorname *m.n.*	forename
Essen *n.n.*	food, meal

Unit 60

bisschen, ein *adj.*	a little
vernünftig *adj.*	sensible
wiederum *adv.*	again
Salon *m.n.*	drawing-room, salon, saloon
realistisch *adj.*	realistic
bewundern	to admire
Fahrkarte *f.n.*	ticket
zitieren	to cite, quote
helfen	to help
Lösung *f.n.*	solution
fürchterlich *adj.*	terrible
Burg (*pl.* Burgen) *f.n.*	castle
jugendlich *adj.*	youthful
wodurch *adv.*	whereby
demokratisch *adj.*	democratic
Wohltat (*pl.* Wohltaten) *f.n.*	kindness
Durchschnitt *m.n.*	average
Alter (*pl.* Alter) *n.n.*	age
Deutsche(r) *f., m.n.*	German (person)
Fernseher (*pl.* Fernseher) *m.n.*	television set

Unit 61

Ursprung *f.n.*	descent, origin
anvertrauen	to entrust
Forst *m.n.*	forest
Text *m.n.*	text
herausbringen	to bring out, publish (a book)
Hafen (*pl.* Häfen) *m.n.*	port
extrem *adj.*	extreme
Milch *f.n.*	milk
Mut *m.n.*	courage
fortan *adv.*	henceforth
Bahnhof (*pl.* Bahnhöfe) *m.n.*	rail station
miteinander *adv.*	together
wiederhören	(telephone) (Auf Wiederhören, till we speak (*lit.* hear) again)
Bau *f.n.*	building, construction
empfindlich *adj.*	sensitive
Moral (*pl.* Moralen) *f.n.*	moral
Flamme *f.n.*	flame
Geschwindigkeit *f.n.*	speed
Revolution *f.n.*	revolution
besonder *adj.*	special, particular

Unit 62

verbringen	to spend (time)
Bus (*pl.* Büsse) *m.n.*	bus
militärisch *adj.*	military
Tat (*pl.* Taten) f.n.	act, deed
umkehren	to return
ernst *adj.*	serious
Foto (*pl.* Fotos) *n.n.*	photograph (also Photographie, *f.n.*)
Vorabend *m.n.*	eve
folglich *adv.*	consequently
weisen	to show
Bier *n.n.*	beer
vorwärts *adv.*	forward(s)
zurücknehmen	to withdraw
Fest *n.n..*	festival
englisch *adj.*	English, (often signifying) British
Werk *n.n.*	factory, work(s)
bezüglich *prep.*	concerning, with regard to
Erregung *f.n.*	excitement
wegwerfen	to throw away
Gedächtnis (*pl.* Gedächtnisse) *n.n.*	memory

Unit 63

stammen (aus)	to be descended (from), come (from)
Rat (*pl.*Räte) *m.n.*	advice, council (lor)
schauen	to look at, observe
Genosse *m.n.* (Genossin, *f.n.*)	colleague, comrade
Menge *n.n.*	crowd
melden (sich)	to report
Funktion *f.n.*	function
schwimmen	to swim
Zug (*pl.* Züge) *m.n.*	feature, train
Notiz (*pl.* Notizen) *f.n.*	note, notice
klatschen	to clap
umgeben	to encircle, surround
erziehen	to bring up
Schauspiel *n.n.*	show, spectacle
Gemeinde *f.n.*	community
leer *adj.*	empty
Bank (*pl.* Bänke) *f.n.*	bank
Erklärung *f.n.*	explanation
typisch *adj.*	typical
Fernsprecher (*pl.* Fernsprecher) *m.n.*	telephone

Unit 64

vergangen *adj.*	past
Basis (*pl.* Basen) *f.n.*	basis
Wirtschaft *f.n.*	economy, housekeeping
Hälfte *f.n.*	half
Erzeugnis (*pl.* Erzeugnisse) *n.n.*	product(ion)
musikalisch *adj.*	musical
Dauer (*pl.* Dauer) *f.n.*	duration, period
beweisen	to prove
blicken	to look
Wunder (*pl.* Wunder) *n.n.*	miracle, wonder
mutig *adj.*	brave
ausstellen	to exhibit
malen	to paint
Besuch *m.n.*	visit
fröhlich *adj.*	cheerful, happy
scharf *adj.*	sharp
Forschung *f.n.*	research
nimmermehr *adv.*	nevermore
Humor *m.n.*	humour
elend *adj.*	miserable

Unit 65

Hilfe *f.n.*	assistance, help
Liebhaber (*pl.* Liebhaber) *m.n.*	lover
Liebhaberin *f.n.*	
Sprache *f.n.*	language, speech
materiell *adj.*	material
feiern	to celebrate
Haut (*pl.* Häute) *f.n.*	skin
mächtig *adj.*	powerful
Ohr (*pl.* Ohren) *n.n.*	ear
telephonieren	to telephone
Meldung *f.n.*	report
beladen	to load
Schlüssel (*pl.* Schlüssel) *m.n.*	key
Offiziell *adj.*	official
adv.	officially
Erziehung *f.n.*	upbringing
Rate *f.n.*	instalment, payment
freilich *adv.*	certainly, of course
Porträt (*pl.* Porträts) *n.n.*	portrait
gelb *adj.*	yellow
rasch *adj.*	rapid, swift
fortgehen	to go away

Unit 66

freundlich *adj.*	friendly
stattfinden	to take place
riskieren	to risk
Stufe *f.n.*	stage, step
zwingen	to force
ruhig *adj.*	calm
populär *adj.*	popular
Satz (*pl.* Sätze) *m.n.*	leap, sentence, set(ting)
anschliessen	to connect
neugierig *adj.*	curious
Serie *f.n.*	series
gefährlich *adj.*	dangerous
Lippe *f.n.*	lip
dünn *adj.*	thin
Durst *m.n.*	thirst
Verhältnis (*pl.* Verhältnisse) *n.n.*	relationship
Operation *f.n.*	operation
Kranke(r) *f., m.n.*	invalid, sick person
freiwillig *adj.*	voluntary
Schutz *m.n.*	protection
kriminell *adj.*	criminal

Unit 67

froh *adj.*	cheerful, glad
Opfer (*pl.* Opfer) *n.n.*	sacrifice, victim
Begierde *f.n.*	desire
Biss (*pl.* Bisse) *m.n.*	bite
Vernunft *f.n.*	reason
tasten	to feel, touch
Regel (*pl.* Regeln) *f.n.*	rule
seither *adv.*	since then
unglücklich *adj.*	unhappy, unfortunate
Illusion *f.n.*	illusion
Tugend (*pl.* Tugenden) *f.n.*	virtue
schätzen	to estimate, value
Verwaltung *f.n.*	administration, management
Wohnung *f.n.*	apartment, flat
Reich *n.n.*	empire, kingdom
Vorsprung *m.n.*	advantage
Qual (*pl.* Qualen) *f.n.*	distress
Mode *f.n.*	fashion
überlassen	to leave
anrufen	to call, ring up

Unit 68

draußen *adv.*	outside
beeinflussen	to influence
überliefern	to deliver
Besucher (*pl.* Besucher) *m.n.*	visitor
Ersatz (*pl.* Ersätze) *m.n.*	substitute
jünger *adj.*	younger
verwenden	to apply, use
Fortschritt *m.n.*	progress
Modell *n.n.*	model
ständig *adj.*	permanent
Rücken (*pl.* Rücken) *m.n.*	back
reservieren	to reserve
international *adj.*	international
spazieren (gehen)	to go for a walk
Haar (*pl.* Haare) *n.n.*	one hair; *pl.* the hair as a whole
befreien	to (set) free
fortfahren	to depart, leave
Maler (*pl.* Maler) *m.n.*	painter
stimmen	to be right, true
Rasse *f.n.*	race
insgesamt *adv.*	altogether

Unit 69

Vorteil *m.n.*	advantage
minder *adj.*	lesser
adv.	less
physisch *adj.*	physical
anordnen	to arrange, command
Form (*pl.* Formen) *f.n.*	form
organisieren	to organise
irren	to err
Waffe *f.n.*	weapon
schmackhaft *adj.*	tasty
erfordern	to call for, require
Sicherheit *f.n.*	certainty, safety
Ladenbesitzer	shopkeeper
(*pl.* Ladenbesitzer) *m.n.*	
merken	to note
vereinigen	to unite
passend *adj.*	suitable
Fürst (*pl.* Fürsten) *m.n.*	prince
vorziehen	to prefer
Technik (*pl.* Techniken) *f.n.*	engineering, technique, technology
Anruf *m.n.*	appeal, call
drinnen *adv.*	inside
Universität	university
(*pl.* Universitäten) *f.n.*	

Unit 70

Tradition *f.n.*	tradition
Phantasie *f.n.*	imagination
lösen	to resolve, solve
Gefängnis (*pl.* Gefängnisse) *n.n.*	imprisonment, prison
Verteidigung *f.n.*	defence
erwidern	to reply
Zivilisation *f.n.*	civilisation
müde *adj.*	tired
Anlass (*pl.* Anlässe) *m.n.*	cause, occasion
vernichten	to destroy
Gebot *n.n.*	order
anschliessend *adj.*	subsequent
braun *adj.*	brown
vorspringen	to leap forward
ausserordentlich *adj.*	extraordinary
Prozent *n.n.*	per cent (*but* Prozentsatz, *m.n.*, percentage)
licht *adj.*	light
heilig *adj.*	holy
Masse *f.n.*	mass (but religious term, Messe *f.n.*)
schützen	to protect
Erzählung *f.n.*	story

Unit 71

Urlaub *m.n.*	leave, vacation
einrichten	to arrange, install
langweilig *adj.*	boring
Ministerium (*pl.* Ministerien) *n.n.*	ministry
ausserhalb *adv., prep.*	outside
Information *f.n.*	piece of information (*pl.* information)
Projekt *n.n.*	project
unbekannt *adj.*	unknown
Auszug (*pl.* Auszüge) *m.n.*	departure, removal
Entwicklung *f.n.*	development
einsam *adj.*	lonely
Anlage *f.n.*	layout, plan
Unterschied *m.n.*	difference
geehrt *adj.*	honoured
Energie *f.n.*	energy
anregen	to stimulate, inspire
Spur *f.n.*	trace, track
mindest *adj.*	least
förderlich *adj.*	beneficial, useful
heiraten	to marry

Unit 72

beschreiben	to describe
Sicherung *f.n.*	protection
ausführen	to carry out
Empfang *m.n.*	reception, welcome, conception
Tote(r) *f., m.n.*	dead (person)
sitzen	to sit
Folge *f.n.*	consequence
Begegnung *f.n.*	encounter, meeting
still *adj.*	quiet, still
offenbar *adj.*	manifest, obvious
sammeln	to collect
Bevölkerung *f.n.*	population
weitergehen	to proceed
Feier (*pl.* Feiern) *f.n.*	festival
beseitigen	to eliminate, remove
täglich *adj.*	daily
Urteil *n.n.*	judgment, verdict
Militär *n.n.*	army, (the) military (singular); soldier (*pl.* Militärs)
rückwärts *adv.*	backwards
Absicht *f.n.*	intention

Unit 73

tanzen	to dance
Datum (*pl.* Daten) *n.n.*	date (in time; the *fruit* is Dattel (*pl.* Datteln) *f.n.*)
empfehlen	to recommend
Kopie *f.n.*	copy
toll *adj.*	mad, wild
Gesang (*pl.* Gesänge) *m.n.*	song
besetzt *adj.*	busy, occupied
abmachen	to arrange, detach
Angebot *n.n.*	offer
vorn *adv.*	in front
Reservierung *f.n.*	reservation (but Schutzgebiet, *n.n.*, nature reserve)
verstossen	to offend
vortreten	to step forward
Anschlüss (*pl.* Anschlüsse) *m.n.*	annexation, connection
verwickeln	to entangle
geeignet *adj.*	suitable
einbrechen	to break in(to)
Abendessen *n.n.*	dinner, supper
erfüllen	to fill
zeichnen	to draw

Unit 74

vergeben	to forgive
gesamt *adj.*	entire, whole
Duft (*pl.* Düfte) *m.n.*	scent
Ausstellung *f.n.*	exhibition
zerstören	to destroy
innerhalb *adv.*	inside
prep.	within
Gefahr (*pl.* Gefahren) *f.n.*	danger
kaum *adv.*	barely
Klima (*pl.* Klimate) *f.n.*	climate
entzwei *adv.*	in two
Wirt(in) *f., m.n.*	host(ess), landlord/landlady
anregend *adj.*	exciting
Königin *f.n.*	queen
Neugier *f.n.*	curiosity
Familienname *m.n.*	surname
Kaufmann (*pl.* Kaufleute) *m.n.*	merchant
vereinigt *adj.*	united
schwören	to swear
fortlaufen	to run away
vorüber *adv.*	past

Unit 75

Kontakt *m.n.*	contact
Stand (*pl.* Stände) *m.n.*	stall, stand
Wurf (*pl.* Würfe) *m.n.*	throw
Reichtum (*pl.* Reichtümer) *m.n.*	riches, wealth
Stil *m.n.*	style
bestens *adv.*	in the best way
mischen	to blend, mix
Einfluss (*pl.* Einflüsse) *m.n.*	influence
Anstalt (*pl.* Anstalten) *f.n.*	institution
Vollendung *f.n.*	completion
gefällig *adj.*	pleasing
knapp *adj.*	scarce, sparse
Gedicht *n.n.*	poem
Maschine *f.n.*	machine
vormals *adv.*	formerly
Geschenk *n.n.*	present
Aussicht *f.n.*	view
klettern	to climb
Mittagessen *n.n.*	lunch(eon)
bewundernswert *adj.*	admirable

Unit 76

Sehen *n.n.*	eye(sight)
Versicherung *f.n.*	insurance
Post (*pl.* Posten) *f.n.*	post(al) service (*but* Postamt *pl.* Postämter, *n.n.* post office)
Ferien (*pl.*) *n.n.*	holiday(s)
erwachen	to wake up
wissentlich *adj.*	conscious
informieren	to inform
eng *adj.*	narrow
küssen	to kiss
vollziehen	to carry out
allezeit *adv.*	always
vorzuziehen *adj.*	preferable
Begriff *m.n.*	concept, idea
teilen	to share
Herstellung *f.n.*	production
verletzen	to injure, offend
befriedigen	to gratify, satisfy
absetzen	to dismiss, set down
üben	to exercise, practise (a trade)
Uhr (*pl.* Uhren) *f.n.*	clock

Unit 77

fassen	to grasp, seize
vorrücken	to advance, move forward
Zeitschrift (*pl.* Zeitschriften) *f.n.*	magazine
umwandeln	to transform
Finger (*pl.* Finger) *m.n.*	finger
Notwendigkeit *f.n.*	necessity
bevölkern	to populate
Tausch *m.n.*	exchange
klingen	to ring, sound
Unfall (*pl.* Unfälle) *m.n.*	accident
stürzen	to fall, rush, overturn
universal *adj.*	universal
Polizei (*pl.* Polizeien) *f.n.*	police
drüben *adv.*	over there
aufmachen	to open
Entscheidung *f.n.*	decision
antasten	to handle, touch
Hut (*pl.* Hüte) *m.n.*	hat
(*pl.* Hut) *f.n.*	protection
verwandeln	to transform

Unit 78

Amt (*pl.* Ämter) *n.n.*	office, post
vorbeigehen	to pass
schmücken	to decorate
Typ *m.n.*	type (person)
Staub *m.n.*	dust
heil *adj.*	safe, whole
Porto (*pl.* Portos) *n.n.*	postage
Lieferant (*pl.* Lieferanten) *m.n.*	supplier
Frühstück *n.n.*	breakfast
vorweg *adv.*	in advance
abgemacht *adj.*	agreed, settled
Eis *n.n.*	ice, ice-cream
Zuname *m.n.*	surname
Mitternacht (*pl.* Mitternächte) *f.n.*	midnight
einladen	to invite
neulich *adv.*	recently
Angelegenheit *f.n.*	business, matter
Gehalt *n.n.*	salary
nachprüfen	to check, verify
Bad (*pl.* Bäder) *n.n.*	bath

Unit 79

Laut *m.n.*	sound
Erfahrung *f.n.*	experience
Meter (*pl.* Meter) *n.n.*	metre
komisch *adj.*	comic
hüten	to guard; sich hüten (vor), to be careful (of)
Sinn *m.n.*	sense
Runde *f.n.*	round (boxing), circle
teils *adv.*	partly
Offizier *m.n.*	officer
paar, ein *adj.*	a few
Anteil *m.n.*	share
verwickelt *adj.*	complicated
Presse *f.n.*	press
unarmen	to embrace
kopieren	to copy
Tanz (*pl.* Tänze) *m.n.*	dance
abschwören	to renounce
Formel (*pl.* Formeln) *f.n.*	formula
wachsen	to grow
fortleben	to survive
Herbst *m.n.*	autumn

Unit 80

befehlen	to command, order
passieren	to happen, pass
Hof (*pl.* Höfe) *m.n.*	court(yard)
erschrecken	to frighten
Truppe *f.n.*	troupe (theatrical); (*pl.* Truppen, military troops)
dankbar *adj.*	grateful
Genie *n.n.*	genius
Länge *f.n.*	length
Besitzer (*pl.* Besitzer) *m.n.*	owner, proprietor
Freundschaft *f.n.*	friendship
Schatten (*pl.* Schatten) *m.n.*	shade, shadow
folgern	to infer
Nachbar (*pl.* Nachbarn) *m.n.* (Nachbarin, *f.n.*)	neighbour
Fernsehen *n.n.*	television
Sturz (*pl.* Stürze) *m.n.*	fall
vermutlich *adv.*	probably
Einladung *f.n.*	invitation
Kilo (*pl.* Kilos) *n.n.*	kilogram(me)
ernennen	to appoint
Verstoss *m.n.*	offence
Nachtisch *m.n.*	dessert, sweet

Unit 81

bauen	to build, grow
total *adj.*	total
aufschlagen	to raise
eindringen	to penetrate
versprechen	to promise
Untersuchung *f.n.*	inspection
tapfer *adj.*	brave
wachen	to be awake
Sammlung *f.n.*	collection
Befehl *m.n.*	command, order
fällen	to cut down
Übung *f.n.*	exercise
Schmuck *m.n.*	jewellery, ornament
Vortrag (*pl.* Vorträge) *m.n.*	lecture, talk
Abmachung *f.n.*	agreement, arrangement
Tuch (*pl.* Tücher) *n.n.*	(piece of) cloth
Beschreibung *f.n.*	description
Kilometer (*pl.* Kilometer) *n.n.*	kilometre
langsam *adj.*	slow
monatlich *adj., adv.*	monthly
Verbrechen *n.n.*	crime

Unit 82

einkaufen	to shop
Direktor (*pl.* Direktoren) *m.n.*	director, headmaster
bisher *adv.*	hitherto
klagen	to complain
Fremde(r) *f., m.n.*	foreigner, stranger
würdig *adj.*	worthy
blitzen	to flash
Rückstand (*pl.* Ruckstände) *m.n.*	remainder, rest (im Rückstand, in arrears)
Ball (*pl.* Bälle) *m.n.*	ball, dance
zurückziehen	to withdraw
positiv *adj.*	positive
Begabung *f.n.*	talent
packen	to grasp, seize
Nachfrage *f.n.*	enquiry
Sitte *f.n.*	custom (Sitten, morals)
vorstehen	to manage
Organisation *f.n.*	organisation
rückwärtsgehen	to decline, go back(wards)
schätzenswert *adj.*	valuable
Möbel (*pl.* Möbel) *n.n.*	furniture

Unit 83

schmerzen	to hurt, pain
Reklame *f.n.*	advertising, publicity
Ferne *f.n.*	distance
vermuten	to suppose
Anwendung *f.n.*	application
wissenschaftlich *adj.*	scientific
Abteilung *f.n.*	department
beiseite *adv.*	aside
Anordnung *f.n.*	arrangement
Stube *f.n.*	chamber, room
Gerät *n.n.*	appliance
verwalten	to administer
fürstlich *adj.*	princely
Sehenswürdigkeit *f.n.*	(tourist) sight
baden	to take a bath
Anwesenheit *f.n.*	presence
ordentlich *adj.*	orderly
Mischung *f.n.*	mixture
wochentlich *adj., adv.*	weekly
Motor (*pl.* Motoren) *m.n.*	engine

Unit 84

einführen	to introduce
Telephon *n.n.*	telephone
vorantwortlich *adj*	responsible
satt *adj.*	satisfied (satt haben, to have had enough)
anklagen	to accuse
Mantel (*pl.* Mäntel) *m.n.*	cloak, coat
Mond *m.n.*	moon
volkreich *adj.*	populous
sichtbar *adj.*	visible
entleihen	to borrow
Insel (*pl.* Inseln) *f.n.*	island
atmen	to breathe
Industrie *f.n.*	industry
vorsetzen	to put forward
Erlebnis (*pl.* Erlebnisse) *n.n.*	experience
loben	to praise
ermässigen	to reduce
offensichtlich *adj.*	obvious
warm *adj.*	warm
lange *adv.*	for a long time

Unit 85

Auskunft (*pl.* Auskünfte) *f.n.*	information
Brauch (*pl.* Bräuche) *m.n.*	custom
aufnehmen	to take up
reparieren	to repair
Büchse *f.n.*	box, can
richten	to arrange, prepare
benutzen	to use
Vorsicht *f.n.*	care, caution
absenden	to send off
Schmerz (*pl.* Schmerzen) *m.n.*	grief, pain
Ausland *m.n.*	abroad
erfahren	to experience
aufschreiben	to write down, note
Geruch (*pl.* Gerüche) *m.n.*	odour
Sitz *m.n.*	seat
versichern	to insure
Schöpfung *f.n.*	creation
hinsetzen, sich	to sit down
preiswert *adj.*	cheap, reasonably-priced
teilnehmen	to participate

Unit 86

ausgehen	to go out
Mannschaft *f.n.*	crew, team
ausziehen	to take off
Heirat (*pl.* Heiraten) *f.n.*	marriage
bequem *adj.*	comfortable
Erwiderung *f.n.*	reply
entstammen	to descend from
Paar *n.n.*	pair
Arbeitnehmer *m.n.*	employee
Lust (*pl.* Lüste) *f.n.*	pleasure (Lust haben, to feel like)
negativ *adj.*	negative
abnehmen	to take off
Experiment *n.n.*	experiment
Leihen	to lend
Marsch (*pl.* Märsche) *m.n.*	march
(*pl.* Marschen) *f.n.*	marsh
bedienen, sich	to help (oneself)
Ziffer (*pl.* Ziffern) *f.n.*	figure (number)
Obst *n.n.*	fruit
Ausländer (*pl.* Ausländer) *m.n.* (Ausländerin, *f.n.*)	foreigner
vorsichtig *adj.*	careful

Unit 87

Gemüse (*pl.* Gemüse) *n.n.*	vegetable
Ausverkauf (*pl.* Ausverkäufe) *m.n.*	sale
Benzin *n.n.*	petrol
Einführung *f.n.*	introduction
Schulter (*pl.* Schultern) *f.n.*	shoulder
unmittelbar *adj.*	immediate
beantworten	to answer
Kuß (*pl.* Küsse) *m.n.*	kiss
begabt *adj.*	talented
Verletzung *f.n.*	injury, offence
begrüßen	to greet
Gewicht *n.n.*	eight
finanziell *adj.*	financial
wahrscheinlich *adj.*	probable
adv.	probably
Mahlzeit (*pl.* Mahlzeiten) *f.n.*	meal
schließlich *adv.*	finally
Meer *n.n.*	sea
gültig *adj.*	valid
Ausstieg *m.n.*	exit
intelligent *adj.*	intelligent

Unit 88

Fluß (*pl.* Flüsse) *m.n.*	river
Auswahl (*pl.* Auswahlen) *f.n.*	selection
Autobahn (*pl.* Autobahnen) *f.n.*	motorway
Neffe *m.n.*	nephew
Blatt (*pl.* Blätter) *n.n.*	leaf
Verantwortung *f.n.*	responsibility
berichten	to report
vorstellen	to introduce, mean (sich vorstellen, to introduce oneself)
ausgeben	to spend
befinden, sich	to be situated
gebrauchen	to use
Hochschule *f.n.*	college
wandern	to walk (hike)
Tasse *f.n.*	cup
einschlafen	to fall asleep
auftreten	to appear, come forward
herrlich *adj.*	magnificent, splendid
Abwesenheit *f.n.*	absence
beliebt *adj.*	popular
Pack (*pl.* Päcke) *m.n.*	pack(et)

Unit 89

viert *adj.*	fourth
Gast (*pl.* Gäste) *m.n.*	guest
liegen	to lie
Großvater (*pl.* Großväter) *m.n.*	grandfather
fangen	to catch
eigen *adj.*	own
betreten	to enter
Onkel (*pl.* Onkel) *m.n.*	uncle
Vorsteher (*pl.* Vorsteher) *m.n.* (Vorsteherin *f.n.*)	manager(ess)
Gegend (*pl.* Gegenden) *f.n.*	region
Ingenieur *m.n.*	engineer
mitteilen	to inform
Katze *f.n.*	cat (*but* Kater, *pl.* Kater, *m.n.*, tom cat)
bestellen	to order
Ei (*pl.* Eier) *n.n.*	egg
freuen, sich	to be pleased (sich freuen auf, to look forward to)
Richter (*pl.* Richter) *m.n.*	judge
fliegen	to fly
Verwicklung *f.n.*	complication

Unit 90

geradeaus	straight ahead
belieben	to like, please
decken	to cover
Kreis *m.n.*	circle
Absender (*pl.* Absender) *m.n.*	sender
kochen	to cook
Fisch *m.n.*	fish
Beamte *m.n.*	official
Kleidung *f.n.*	clothing
Medizin (*pl.* Medizinen) *f.n.*	medicine
pensioniert *adj.*	retired
ausländisch *adj.*	foreign
hinlegen	to put down (sich hinlegen, to lie down)
grossartig *adj.*	great
Bibliothek (*pl.* Bibliotheken) *f.n.*	library
Imbiss *m.n.*	snack
Erwachsene *m., f.n.*	adult
Bein *n.n.*	bone, leg
Chemie *f.n.*	chemistry
durchfallen *f.n.*	to fail

Unit 91

verheiraten	to marry
Mauer (*pl.* Mauern) *f.n.*	wall
ansagen	to announce
Hügel (*pl.* Hügel) *m.n.*	hill
Atelier (*pl.* Ateliers) *n.n.*	studio
benehmen, sich	to behave (benehmen, to take away)
Kasse *f.n.*	cashier's desk, till
Aufführung *f.n.*	performance
Religion (*pl.* Religionen) *f.n.*	religion
Miete *f.n.*	rent
Trupp (*pl.* Trupps) *m.n*	gang, troop
Zufall (*pl.* Zufälle) *m.n.*	accident
fortdauern	to continue
Krankenhaus (*pl.* Krankenhäuser) *n.n.*	hospital
parken	to park
schneiden	to cut
Flug (*pl.* Flüge) *m.n.*	flight
Gespräch *n.n.*	conversation
Eisenbahn (*pl.* Eisenbahnen) *f.n.*	railway
beeilen, sich	to hurry

Unit 92

Einwohner (*pl.* Einwohner) *m.n.*	inhabitant
arbeitslos *adj.*	unemployed
Gebirge *pl. n.n.*	mountains
Koffer (*pl.* Koffer) *m.n.*	suitcase
Motorrad (*pl.* Motorräder) *n.n.*	motor-cycle
Tante *f.n.*	aunt
Gramm *n.n.*	gram(me)
Vorstellung *f.n.*	introduction
einstürzen	to collapse
Adresse *f.n.*	address
Frucht (*pl.* Früchte) *f.n.*	fruit
achten (auf)	to pay attention (to)
Lied (*pl.* Lieder) *n.n.*	song
Zweck *m.n.*	purpose
Ausflug (*pl.* Ausflüge) *m.n.*	excursion
besorgen	to obtain, see to
Böse *n.n.*	evil
regnen	to rain
Gebäude (*pl.* Gebäude) *n.n.*	building
Stahl *m.n.*	steel

Unit 93

Heimat *f.n.*	homeland
erreichen	to reach
Polizist (*pl.* Polizisten) *m.n.*	policeman
Anzug (*pl.*Anzüge) *m.n.*	suit
raten	to advise, guess
Hähnchen (*pl.* Hähnchen) *n.n.*	chicken
leise *adj., adv.*	slow(ly)
Kartoffel (*pl.* Kartoffeln) *f.n.*	potato
Rundfunk *m.n.*	broadcasting, radio
Grenze *f.n.*	boundary, frontier
Ausdruck (*pl.* Ausdrücke) *m.n.*	expression
Geburt (*pl.* Geburten) *f.n.*	birth
regelmäßig *adj., adv.*	regular(ly)
Aufenthalt *m.n.*	stay
Küche *f.n.*	kitchen
bedeckt *adj.*	covered
Freizeit *f.n.*	leisure (time)
besichtigen	to view
Lebensmittel *pl. n.n.*	groceries
Geist (*pl.* Geister) *m.n.*	ghost, spirit

Unit 94

verleihen	to lend
rosa *adj.*	pink
ehrlich *adj.*	honest
Schuh *m.n.*	shoe
Anschrift *f.n.*	address
wehtun	to hurt
Paß (*pl.* Pässe) *m.n.*	passport
Verbindung *f.n.*	contact
probieren	to try
Badezimmer (*pl.* Badezimmer) *n.n.*	bathroom
grau *adj.*	grey
ledig *adj.*	unmarried
eilen	to hurry
Rassist (*pl.* Rassisten) *m.n.* (Rassistin, *f.n.*)	racist
befriedigend *adj.*	satisfactory
männlich *adj.*	masculine
erlauben	to allow
Nichte *f.n.*	niece
Gastgeber (*pl.* Gastgeber) *m.n.*	host
heizen	to heat

Unit 95

klopfen	to knock
Einstieg *m.n.*	entrance
Bedienung *f.n.*	service
jährlich *adj.*	annual
Grossmutter (*pl.* Grossmütter) *f.n.*	grandmother
stolz *adj.*	proud
Armut *f.n.*	poverty
höflich *adj.*	polite
verbessern	to improve
Bezirk *m.n.*	area, district
deutlich *adj., adv.*	clear(ly)
abhängen (von)	to depend (on)
Eigentum (*pl.* Eigentümer) *n.n.*	property
kriegerisch *adj.*	warlike
rauchen	to smoke
fleißig *adj.*	industrious
bunt *adj.*	colourful
wecken	to wake
schade *adv.*	a pity (wie schade! what a shame!)
vorhaben	to intend

Unit 96

Ermäßigung *f.n.*	reduction
Schrift (*pl.* Schriften) *f.n.*	writing
Hose *f.n.*	trousers
Käse *m.n.*	cheese
Tasche *f.n.*	bag, pocket
erschaffen	to create
Beweis *m.n.*	proof
Kassette *f.n.*	cassette
Abendbrot *n.n.*	supper
Doppel (*pl.* Doppel) *n.n.*	duplicate
Magen (*pl.* Mägen) *m.n.*	stomach
vortrefflich *adj.*	excellent
Butter *f.n.*	butter
Passagier *m.n.*	passenger
anziehen, sich	to get dressed
Sport *m.n.*	sport
Zuschauer (*pl.* Zuschauer) *m.n.*	spectator
umziehen	to move house (sich umziehen, to change clothes)
Liter (*pl.* Liter) *n.n.*	litre
Vetter (*pl.* Vetter) *m.n.*	cousin

Unit 97

Kunde *m.n.*	customer
weiblich *adj.*	feminine
Gepäck *n.n.*	luggage
dreckig *adj.*	dirty
einschließlich *adj.*	inclusive
Handtasche *f.n.*	handbag
Belieben *n.n.*	pleasure
Fahrrad (*pl.* Fahrräder) *n.n.*	bicycle
abholen	to fetch
verletzt *adj.*	injured
Brust (*pl.* Brüste) *f.n.*	breast, chest
Hemd (*pl.* Hemden) *n.n.*	shirt
Bruch (*pl.* Brüche) *m.n.*	break
Video (*pl.* Videos) *n.n.*	video
hold *adj.*	charming, gracious
Anregung *f.n.*	excitement
genannt *adj.*	named
schuld(ig) *adj.*	guilty
Träne *f.n.*	tear
Größe *f.n.*	quantity, size

Unit 98

wach *adj.*	awake
Haustier *n.n.*	pet
religiös *adj.*	religious
blöd *adj.*	stupid
Gaststätte *f.n.*	restaurant
sparen	to save (money)
ärztlich *adj.*	medical
Rock (*pl.* Röcke) *m.n.*	jacket, skirt
horchen	to listen (to)
Computer (*pl.* Computer) *m.n.*	computer
treu *adj.*	faithful, loyal
Reihe *f.n.*	row
lehren	to teach
umsonst *adv.*	free of charge, in vain
Zigarette *f.n.*	cigarette
Verkehr *m.n.*	traffic
weich *adj.*	soft
großzügig *adj.*	generous
einschreiben	to enrol, register
irgendwo *adv.*	somewhere

Unit 99

füllen	to fill
Biologie *f.n.*	biology
Fußgänger *m.n.*	pedestrian
umsteigen	to change (transport)
naß *adj.*	wet
elektrisch *adj.*	electric(al)
kaputt *adj.*	broken
Holz (*pl.* Hölzer) *n.n.*	wood
lehnen	to lean, rest
Reisende *m., f.n.*	traveller
Apfel (*pl.* Äpfel) *m.n.*	apple
Norm (*pl.* Normen) *f.n.*	norm, rule, standard
verpassen	to miss (transport)
zufrieden *adj.*	content(ed)
Physik *f.n.*	physics
Bleistift *m.n.*	pencil
einverstanden *adj.*	agreed
kostbar *adj.*	costly
Lektüre *f.n.*	reading (matter)
Mehrheit *f.n.*	majority

Unit 100

Entwurf (*pl.* Entwürfe) *m.n.*	design, plan
darlegen	to explain
Betrieb *m.n.*	business, firm
Quittung *f.n.*	receipt
blaß *adj.*	pale
Lehre *f.n.*	teaching
vergehen	to pass
besorgt *adj.*	worried
Philosophie *f.n.*	philosophy
Minderheit *f.n.*	minority
kleben	to stick
bestimmen	to determine, fix
verfassen	to compose, write
Teller *m.n.*	plate
beschweren, sich	to complain
überfallen	to attack, overtake
entstehen	to arise, originate
jagen	to hunt
grausam *adj.*	cruel
österreichisch *adj.*	Austrian

German Index

Besuch 64
besuchen 58
Besucher 68
Betrag 41
betreffen 39
betreten 89
Betrieb 100
Bett 46
bevölkern 77
Bevölkerung 72
bevor 11
bewachen 39
bewahren 36
bewegen 16
Bewegung 23
Beweis 96
beweisen 64
bewohnen 59
bewundern 60
bewundernswert 75
bezahlen 6
bezeichnen 50
beziehen 47
Bezirk 95
bezüglich 62
Bibliothek 90
Bier 62
bieten 13
Bild 33
bilden 32
billig 34
Biologie 99
bis 5
bisher 82
Biss 67
bisschen 60
bitte 33
bitten 23
blass 100
Blatt 88
blau 38
bleiben 9
Bleistift 99
Blick 34
blicken 64
Blitz 47
blitzen 82

blöd 98
bloss 33
Blume 30
Blut 57
Boden 59
Boot 56
Böse 92
bös(e) 21
Brauch 85
brauchen 39
braun 70
brechen 32
breit 26
Brief 32
bringen 20
Brot 59
Bruch 97
Bruder 34
Brust 97
Buch 19
Büchse 85
Bundesrepublik 26
Bundestag 42
bunt 95
Burg 60
Bus 62
Butter 96

Café 56
Chemie 90
Computer 98

da 6
dabei 13
dadurch 24
dafür 11
dagegen 15
daher 21
dahin 26
dahinter 34
damals 29
Dame 15
damit 8
danach 21
daneben 31

Dank 32
dankbar 80
danken 11
dann 9
daran 12
darauf 11
daraus 21
darein 27
darin 13
darlegen 100
darstellen 26
darüber 23
darum 20
darunter 29
das 1
Dasein 31
dass 1
dasselbe 4
Datum 73
Dauer 64
dauern 31
davon 24
dazu 20
decken 90
dein 4
demokratisch 60
Denken 37
denken 10
denn 7
der 1
deuten 41
deutlich 95
Deutsch 6
deutsch 15
Deutsche(r) 60
Deutschland 38
Dichter 43
dick 21
die 1
dienen 20
Dienst 24
diese 1
dieselbe 4
dieser 1
dieses 1
Ding 9
direkt 49

Direktor 82
dirigieren 51
doch 7
Doktor 42
Doppel 96
Dorf 41
dort 7
dreckig 97
drehen 33
drinnen 69
dritt 35
drüben 77
Druck 58
drücken 28
dunkel 32
dünn 66
durch 5
durchfallen 90
Durchfahrt 49
Durchschnitt 60
dürfen 5
Durst 66

eben 7
ebenso 40
echt 35
Eck 58
Ehe 36
Ehre 33
ehrlich 94
Ei 89
eigen 89
Eigenschaft 57
eigentlich 26
Eigentum 95
Eile 55
eilen 94
eilig 40
ein(e) 1
einander 55
einbrechen 73
eindringen 81
Eindruck 36
einfach 30
Einfluss 75
einführen 84

Einführung 87
Eingang 24
eingehen 46
eingehend 48
Einheit 56
einiger 5
Einkauf 47
einkaufen 82
einkommen 47
einladen 78
Einladung 80
einmal 19
einrichten 71
einsam 71
einschlafen 88
einschliessen 37
einschliesslich 97
einschreiben 98
einsteigen 51
Einstieg 95
einstürzen 92
eintreten 16
Eintritt 27
einverstanden 99
Einwohner 92
Einzelheit 49
einzig 47
Eis 78
Eisen 48
Eisenbahn 91
elektrisch 99
Element 53
Elend 58
elend 64
Eltern 36
Empfang 72
empfangen 14
empfehlen 73
empfindlich 61
empor 37
Ende 18
endlich 10
Energie 71
eng 76
englisch 62
entdecken 25
entgehen 58

enthalten 43
entkommen 44
entlang 10
entleihen 84
entscheiden 38
Entscheidung 77
entschuldigen 33
Entschuldigung 57
entstammen 86
entstehen 100
entwickeln 21
Entwicklung 71
Entwurf 100
entzückend 46
entzwei 74
er 1
Erde 15
erfahren 85
Erfahrung 79
Erfolg 40
erfolgreich 43
erfordern 69
erfüllen 73
Ergebnis 33
ergreifen 41
erhalten 22
erholen 19
erinnern 14
Erinnerung 25
erkennen 17
erklären 35
Erklärung 63
erlauben 94
erleben 59
Erlebnis 84
ermässigen 84
Ermässigung 96
ernennen 80
ernst 62
erregen 54
erregt 58
Erregung 62
erreichen 93
Ersatz 68
erschaffen 96
Erscheinen 50
erscheinen 24

erschrecken 80
ersetzen 38
erst 9
erstaunen 45
erwachen 76
Erwachsene 90
erwidern 70
Erwiderung 86
erzählen 35
Erzählung 70
Erzeugnis 64
erziehen 63
Erziehung 65
es 1
Essen 59
essen 14
etwa 27
etwas 20
europäisch 46
existieren 22
Experiment 86
extrem 61

Fabrik 44
Fach 23
fähig 44
fahren 8
Fahrkarte 60
Fahrrad 97
Fahrt 37
Fall 14
fallen 19
fällen 81
falls 15
falsch 49
Familie 24
Familienname 74
fangen 89
Farbe 31
fassen 77
fast 25
fehlen 25
Fehler 26
Feier 72
feiern 65
fein 43

Feind 49
Feld 34
Fenster 51
Ferien 76
fern 16
Ferne 83
Fernsehen 80
Fernseher 60
Fernsprecher 63
fertig 26
Fest 62
fest 42
festmachen 46
feststellen 44
Feuer 25
Figur 41
Film 16
finanziell 87
finden 6
Finger 77
Firma 38
Fisch 90
Flamme 61
Fleisch 49
fleissig 95
fliegen 89
Flug 91
Flugzeug 50
Fluss 88
Folge 72
folgen 12
folgend 47
folgern 80
folglich 62
förderlich 71
fordern 25
Form 69
Formel 79
Forschung 64
Forst 61
fort 6
fortan 61
fortdauern 91
fortfahren 68
fortgehen 65
fortlaufen 74
fortleben 79

Fortschritt 68
fortsetzen 18
Foto(graphie) 62
Frage 12
fragen 9
französisch 44
Frau 8
Fräulein 34
frei 19
Freiheit 37
freilich 65
freiwillig 66
Freizeit 93
fremd 25
Fremde(r) 82
Freude 35
freuen 89
Freund 12
freundlich 66
Freundschaft 80
Friede(n) 32
frisch 56
Frist 55
froh 67
fröhlich 64
Frucht 92
früh 18
früher 31
Frühling 54
Frühstück 78
fühlen 18
führen 27
füllen 99
Funktion 63
für 2
fürchten 53
Fürst 69
fürstlich 83
Fuss 21
Fussgänger 99

ganz 4
gar nicht 24
Garten 50
Gast 89
Gastgeber 94

Gaststätte 98
Gatte 48
gebären 34
Gebäude 92
geben 7
Gebiet 28
Gebirge 92
Gebot 70
gebrauchen 88
Geburt 93
Gedächtnis 62
Gedanke 50
Gedicht 75
geehrt 71
geeignet 73
Gefahr 74
gefährlich 66
gefallen 21
gefällig 75
Gefängnis 70
Gefühl 53
gegen 11
Gegend 89
Gegenstand 23
Gegenteil 26
gegenüber 12
Gegenwart 49
gegenwärtig 45
Gehalt 78
geheim 56
Geheimnis 52
gehen 5
gehören 36
Geist 93
gelangen 37
gelb 65
Geld 22
Gelegenheit 44
gelegentlich 23
gelten 24
gemein 33
Gemeinde 63
Gemüse 87
genannt 97
genau 19
General 58
Genie 80

Genosse 63
genug 9
genügen 19
geöffnet 56
Geographie 57
Gepäck 97
gerade 19
geradeaus 90
Gerät 83
gerecht 59
Gerechtigkeit 48
gering 36
gern(e) 15
Geruch 85
gesamt 74
Gesang 73
Geschäft 16
geschehen 23
Geschichte 28
Geschenk 75
geschlossen 53
Geschmack 35
Geschwindigkeit 61
gesellig 51
Gesellschaft 15
Gesetz 47
Gesicht 24
Gespräch 91
Gestalt 23
gestatten 10
gestern 28
gesund 54
Gesundheit 59
Getränk 34
gewähren 53
Gewicht 87
gewinnen 45
gewiss 19
Gewissen 49
gewissenhaft 56
Gewissheit 52
gewöhnen 39
Gewohnheit 40
gewöhnlich 38
glänzend 49
Glas 45
Glaube 50

glauben k7
gleich 26
Glück 46
glücklich 17
Gold 36
Gott 19
Gramm 92
grau 94
grausam 100
greifen 54
Grenze 93
gross 5
grossartig 90
Grösse 97
Grossmutter 95
Grossvater 89
grosszügig 98
grün 36
Grund 15
gründen 42
Grundsatz 39
Gruppe 38
Gruss 39
grüssen 37
gültig 47
Gunst 59
gut 3
Güte 30

Haar 68
haben 1
Hafen 61
Hähnchen 93
halb 31
Hälfte 64
Halt 54
halten 9
Hand 14
Handel 36
handeln 10
Handtasche 97
hart 32
Haupt 35
hauptsächlich 51
Haus 10
Haustier 98

kein 2
kennen 8
kennenlernen 52
Kenntnis 51
Kerl 35
Kilo 80
Kilometer 81
Kind 10
Kino 55
Kirche 34
klagen 82
klar 33
Klasse 30
klatschen 63
kleben 100
Kleid 35
Kleidung 90
klein 6
klettern 75
klingen 77
klopfen 95
klug 49
Knabe 33
knapp 75
kochen 90
Koffer 92
komisch 79
kommen 5
Kommerz 54
König 30
Königin 74
können 3
Kontakt 75
Kopf 12
Kopie 73
kopieren 79
Körper 17
Kost 27
kostbar 99
Kraft 14
krank 51
Kranke(r) 66
Krankenhaus 91
Krankheit 53
Kreis 90
kreuzen 44
Krieg 11

kriegen 37
kriegerisch 95
kriminell 66
Krise 57
Küche 93
kühl 58
Kunde 97
Kunst 17
Künstler 42
kurz 31
Kuss 87
küssen 76

lächeln 48
lachen 43
Laden 28
Ladenbesitzer 69
Lage 27
Land 14
Landschaft 47
lang 13
lange 84
Länge 80
längs 18
langsam 81
langweilig 71
Lärm 58
lärmen 55
lassen 8
laufen 26
Laut 79
laut 36
Leben 9
leben 12
lebendig 38
Lebensmittel 93
ledig 94
leer 63
legen 7
lehnen 99
Lehre 100
lehren 98
Lehrer(in) 51
leicht 17
Leid 55
leid 58

Leidenschaft 52
leider 52
leihen 86
leise 93
leisten 25
leiten 34
Lektüre 99
lernen 16
Lesen 55
lesen 18
letzt 10
Leute 14
Licht 25
licht 70
lieb 20
Liebe 13
lieben 10
lieber 33
Liebhaber 65
Lied 92
Lieferant 78
liefern 58
liegen 89
Linie 24
link 44
links 15
Lippe 66
Liter 96
loben 84
los 20
lösen 70
Lösung 60
Luft 20
Lust 86

machen 3
Macht 34
mächtig 65
Mädchen 16
Magen 96
Mahlzeit 87
Mal 7
malen 64
Maler 68
man 2
manchmal 42

108

Mann 5	mitbringen 44	Nachmittag 20
männlich 94	miteinander 61	nachprüfen 78
Mannschaft 86	Mitglied 47	Nachricht(en) 55
Mantel 84	mitkommen 38	nächst 45
Mark 26	Mittag 18	Nacht 12
Markt 48	Mittagessen 75	Nachtisch 80
Marsch 86	Mitte 22	nackt 53
marschieren 44	mitteilen 89	nah(e) 12
Maschine 75	Mittel 19	Nähe 40
Mass 27	mitten 31	näher 54
Masse 70	Mitternacht 78	nähern 59
materiell 65	mittlerweile 44	Name 12
Mauer 91	Möbel 82	Nase 97
Medizin 90	Mode 67	nass 99
Meer 87	Modell 68	national 51
mehr 2	modern 51	Natur 27
mehrere 19	mögen 36	natürlich 9
Mehrheit 99	möglich 11	neben 24
mein 3	Moment 10	Neffe 88
meinen 27	Monat 14	negativ 86
Meinung 55	monatlich 81	nehmen 6
Meister 19	Mond 84	Neid 54
melden 63	Moral 61	nein 7
Meldung 65	moralisch 48	nennen 16
Menge 63	Morgen 13	neu 9
Mensch 19	morgen 23	Neugier 74
menschlich 24	Motor 83	neugierig 60
merken 69	Motorrad 92	neulich 78
Messe 70	müde 70	niedrig 31
Meter 79	Mühe 30	nicht 1
Methode 51	Mund 53	Nichte 94
Miete 91	Musik 35	nichts 6
mieten 47	musikalisch 64	nie(mals) 7
Milch 61	müssen 5	niemand 41
mild 42	Mut 61	nimmer 56
Militär 72	mutig 64	nimmermehr 64
militärisch 62	Mutter 20	noch 4
minder 69		Nord(en) 49
Minderheit 100		Norm 99
mindest 71	**na 14**	Not 31
Minister 41	nach 7	nötig 11
Ministerium 71	Nachbar(in) 80	Notiz 51
Minute 29	nachdem 9	notwendigkeit 77
mischen 75	nachdenken 50	Null 13
Mischung 83	nachfolgen 50	null 52
Misserfolg 56	Nachfrage 82	Nummer 18
mit 23	nachher 27	nun 8

sie 1
Silber 35
singen 48
Sinn 79
Sitte 82
Sitz 85
sitzen 72
so 6
sobald 43
sofort 47
sogar 20
Sohn 17
solang(e) 40
Soldat 45
sollen 4
Sommer 41
sonderbar 59
sondern 13
Sonne 22
sonst 59
Sorge 43
sorgen 38
Sorgfalt 50
Sorte 49
soviel 24
sparen 98
Spass 25
spät 20
später 58
spazieren(gehen) 68
Speise 27
speisen 28
Spiel 24
spielen 15
Sport 96
Sprache 65
sprechen 8
Spur 71
Staat 18
Stadt 12
Stahl 92
stammen 63
Stand 75
ständig 68
stark 19
statt 21
stattfinden 66

Staub 78
stecken 19
stehen 4
steigen 19
Stein 44
Stelle 49
stellen 5
Stellung 56
sterben 21
Stern 46
Stil 75
still 72
Stimme 21
stimmen 68
Stirn 57
Stock 59
Stoff 45
stolz 95
Strasse 21
strecken 51
streng 39
Strom 42
Stube 83
Stück 6
Student 29
studieren 50
Stufe 66
Stuhl 35
Stunde 8
Sturz 80
stürzen 77
stützen 49
suchen 10
Süd(en) 52
süss 32
sympathisch 67
System 42
Szene 40

Tafel 51
Tag 7
täglich 72
Tante 92
Tanz 79
tanzen 79
tapfer 81

Tasche 96
Tasse 88
tasten 67
Tat 62
tätig 52
Tätigkeit 57
tatsächlich 18
Tausch 77
Technik 69
Tee 39
Teil 14
teilen 76
teilnehmen 85
teils 79
Telephon 84
telephonieren 65
Teller 100
teuer 22
Text 61
Theater 48
tief 29
Tier 43
Tisch 23
Titel 42
Tochter 17
Tod 22
toll 73
tot 52
total 81
Tote(r) 72
töten 53
Tradition 70
tragen 14
Träne 97
Traum 47
träumen 22
traurig 47
treffen 20
treiben 26
trennen 59
Treppe 95
treu 98
trinken 39
trocken 58
trotz 17
Trupp 91
Truppe 80

112

Tuch 81
Tugend 67
tun 3
Tür 16
Typ 78
typisch 63

üben 76
über 8
überall 22
übereinstimmen 40
Übereinstimmung 39
überfallen 100
überhaupt 48
überholen 57
überlassen 67
überlegen 33
überliefern 68
überraschen 55
Überraschung 53
übrigens 26
Übung 81
Uhr 76
um 6
umarmen 79
umgeben 63
umher 52
umkehren 62
umsonst 98
Umstand 49
umsteigen 99
umwandeln 77
umziehen 96
unbekannt 71
und 1
Unfall 77
ungefähr 41
ungeheuer 46
ungewöhnlich 40
unglücklich 67
universal 77
Universität 69
unmittelbar 87
unmöglich 24
unser 4
unten 18

unter 7
Unterhalt 56
unterhalten 55
Unterhaltung 58
unterscheiden 40
Unterschied 71
untersuchen 40
Untersuchung 81
unwissend 36
Urlaub 71
Ursprung 61
Urteil 72
urteilen 32

Vater 16
Verantwortung 88
verbessern 95
verbinden 44
Verbindung 94
verboten 21
Verbrechen 81
verbringen 62
verdienen 52
Verein 56
vereinbar 55
vereinigen 69
vereinigt 74
verfassen 100
Verfasser 54
verfolgen 41
vergangen 64
Vergangenheit 48
vergeben 74
vergehen 100
vergessen 19
Vergnügen 24
vergrössern 52
Verhalten 48
Verhältnis 66
verheiraten 91
verhindern 23
Verkauf 40
verkaufen 31
Verkehr 98
verlangen 38
verlassen 25

verleihen 94
verletzen 76
verletzt 97
Verletzung 87
verlieren 20
verloren 56
vermeiden 51
vermieten 44
vermindern 55
vermuten 83
vernichten 70
Vernunft 67
vernünftig 60
verpassen 99
verpflichten 56
verrückt 57
verschieden 29
verschwinden 43
versichern 85
Versicherung 76
versprechen 81
Verstand 43
verstecken 55
verstehen 11
Verstoss 80
verstossen 73
Versuch 57
versuchen 26
verteidigen 42
Verteidigung 70
Vertrauen 41
vertrauen 38
vertreten 33
Vertreter(in) 43
verwalten 83
Verwaltung 67
verwandeln 77
Verwandte(r) 40
verwenden 68
verwickeln 73
verwickelt 79
Verwicklung 89
verwirklichen 39
verzeihen 32
Verzeihung 42
Vetter 96
Video 97

viel(e) 8
vielleicht 11
Viereck 57
viereckig 45
viert 89
Viertel 53
Vogel 42
Volk 21
volkreich 84
voll 15
vollenden 29
Vollendung 75
völlig 28
vollkommen 27
vollständig 38
vollziehen 76
von 1
vor 4
Vorabend 62
voran 53
vorantwortlich 84
voraus 54
voraussagen 56
vorbei 46
vorbeigehen 78
vorbereiten 36
vorder 18
vorerst 57
Vorfall 37
vorhaben 95
vorher 26
vorhergehend 55
vorhin 28
vorig 19
vormals 75
Vormittag 56
vormittags 46
vorn 73
Vorname 59
vornehm 54
vorrücken 77
Vorschlag 53
vorschlagen 45
vorsetzen 84
Vorsicht 85
vorsichtig 86
vorspringen 70

Vorsprung 67
vorstehen 82
Vorsteher(in) 89
vorstellen 88
Vorstellung 92
Vorteil 69
Vortrag 81
vortrefflich 96
vortreten 73
vorüber 74
vorwärts 62
vorweg 78
vorziehen 69
vorzuziehen 76

wach 98
wachen 81
wachsen 79
Waffe 69
Wagen 45
wagen 50
Wahl 53
wählen 50
wahr 14
während 9
Wahrheit 30
wahrscheinlich 87
Wald 34
Wand 39
wandern 88
wann 6
warm 84
warten 13
warum 16
was 3
waschen 39
Wasser 13
wechseln 24
wecken 95
weder...noch 9
Weg 22
weg 43
wegen 9
wegwerfen 62
Weh 57
weh 52

wehtun 94
weiblich 97
weich 98
weil 8
Wein 47
weinen 54
Weise 22
weisen 62
weiss 16
weit 12
weiter 47
weitergehen 72
welcher 5
Welt 10
wenig 6
weniger 34
wenn 4
wer 5
werden 2
werfen 28
Werk 62
Wert 22
wert 28
Wesen 41
West(en) 55
Wetter 34
wichtig 27
Wichtigkeit 37
wider 13
widersprechen 46
wie 2
wieder 13
wiederbringen 59
wiederholen 32
wiederhören 61
wiederkehren 58
wiedersehen 9
wiederum 60
wieviel(e) 9
Wille(n) 46
Wind 32
Winter 40
wir 3
wirklich 10
Wirklichkeit 31
Wirt(in) 74
Wirtschaft 64

English Index

117

crime 81
criminal 66
crisis 57
cross, to 44
crowd 63
cruel 100
cry 44
cry, to 46
cup 88
curiosity 74
curious 53, 66
current 41, 42
custom 40, 82, 85
customer 97
cut 52
cut, to 91
cut down, to 81

daily 72
dance 79, 82
dance, to 73
danger 74
dangerous 66
dare, to 50
dark 32
darling 42
date 73
daughter 17
day 7
dead 52
dead (person) 72
deal 16
dear 20, 22
dearer 33
death 22
debt 31
decide, to 38
decision 77
declare, to 35
decline, to 82
decorate, to 78
deed 62
deep 29
defence 70
defend, to 42
delicate 51

delight 35
deliver, to 68
demand, to 25, 38
democratic 60
depart, to 22, 68
department 83
departure 36, 71
depend (on), to 95
descend, to 34, 46
descend from, to 86
descended from, to be 63
descent 61
describe, to 72
description 81
design 100
designate, to 50
desire 67
desire, to 50
dessert 80
destiny 59
destroy, to 70, 74
detach, to 73
detail 49
determine, to 100
develop, to 21
development 71
die, to 21
difference 71
different 25, 29
difficult 37
difficulty 30
dine, to 28
dinner 73
direct 49
direct, to 51
direction 30
directly 19
director 82
dirty 97
disagreeable 58
disappear, to 43
discover, to 25
discuss, to 23
disease 53
dismiss, to 76
distance 83
distant 16

distinguish, to 40
distinguished 54
distress 67
district 53, 95
do, to 3, 25
do good, to 52
doctor 42, 44
dog 36
domain 51
door 16
doubt 17
doubt, to 42
down, to put 90
downwards 28, 29
draw, to 18, 73
drawing-room 60
dream 47
dream, to 22
dress 35
dressed, to get 96
drink 34
drink, to 39
drive, to 26
dry 58
duplicate 96
duration 64
during 9
dust 78
duty 50, 59
dwell, to 11

each 2
each other 55
ear 65
earlier 31
early 18
earn, to 52
earth 15
east 54
easy 17
eat, to 14, 28
economic 38
economy 64
edge 34
educate, to 32
egg 89

120

true 14
true, to be 68
true, to come 39
trust 41
truth 30
try, to 26, 94
turn, to 12, 33
turn off, to 28
turn on, to 26
two, in 74
type 78
typical 63

unassisted, 41
uncle 89
under 7
under it 29
undergo, to 59
underneath 18
understand, to 11
understanding 43
unemployed 92
unfortunate 67
unfortunately 52
unhappy 67
unit 56
unite, to 69
united 74
unity 56
universal 77
university 69
unknown 71
unmarried 94
unusual 40
up, to bring 63
up here 23
up to 5, 27, 48
upbringing 65
upon 2
upper 23
upwards 28, 31, 37
use 35
use, to 68, 85, 88
use, to be of 14
useful, 37, 21
useful, to be 14

useless 41
usual 38

vacate, to 25
vacation 71
vain, in 98
valid 87
valuable 82
value 22
value, to 67
vegetable 87
verdict 72
verify, to 78
very 4
vicinity 40
victim 67
video 97
view 75
view, to 93
village 41
virtue 67
visible 84
visit 64
visit, to 58
visitor 68
voice 21
voluntary 66

wait for, to 13
wake, to 95
wake up, to 76
walk, to 26, 88
walk, to go for a 68
wall 39, 91
want, to 6, 20
want to, to 86
war 11
warlike 95
warm 84
wash, to 39
water 13
way 22
way, by the 26
way, in the best 75
way, this 30

we 3
weak 50
wealth 75
weapon 69
weather 34
wedding 49
week 27
weekly 83
weep, to 54
weight 87
welcome 72
well 3, 8, 54
west 55
wet 99
what 3
what, about 30
wheel 26
when 5, 6
where 3
whereby 57, 60
whether 50
which 5
which, from 52
which, of 52
which, on 30
which, with 32
white 16
who 5
whole 28, 74, 78
wholly 28
why 16
wide 12
wife 8
wild 73
will 46
win, to 45
wind 32
window 51
wine 47
winter 40
wish 43
wish, to 6, 20
with 2, 6
with that 8
with which 32
withdraw, to 62, 82
within 16, 74

130

BOOKS FROM OLEANDER

A LIFETIME'S READING
Philip Ward

CONTEMPORARY GERMAN POETRY: AN ANTHOLOGY
Trans. by Ewald Osers

WITH MY OWN WINGS: MEMOIRS
Raymond Lister

INDIAN MANSIONS: A SOCIAL HISTORY OF THE HAVELI
Sarah Tillotson

THE HIDDEN MUSIC: SELECTED POEMS
Östen Sjöstrand

BULGARIAN VOICES: LETTING THE PEOPLE SPEAK
Philip Ward

BULGARIA: A TRAVEL GUIDE
Philip Ward

SOFIA: PORTRAIT OF A CITY
Philip Ward

GREGUERIAS: THE WIT AND WISDOM OF
Ramón Gómez de la Serna

LOST SONGS: POEMS
Philip Ward

SWANSONGS: POEMS
Sue Lenier

RAIN FOLLOWING: NEW POEMS
Sue Lenier

RAJASTHAN, AGRA DELHI: A TRAVEL GUIDE
Philip Ward

SOUTH INDIA: A TRAVEL GUIDE
Philip Ward

WESTERN INDIA: A TRAVEL GUIDE
Philip Ward

GUJARAT, DAMAN, DIU: A TRAVEL GUIDE
Philip Ward

FATHER GANDER'S NURSERY RHYMES
Per Gander

SUDAN TALES: REMINISCENCES OF BRITISH WIVES
Rosemary Kenrick